Designing Home Interiors

A Study Guide

Second Edition

COAST COMMUNITY COLLEGE DISTRICT
Costa Mesa, California

RANCHO SANTIAGO COMMUNITY COLLEGE DISTRICT
Santa Ana, California

Revised by Judy Hamilton

Bellwether Press

A Division of Burgess International Group, Inc.

Coast Community College District

David A. Brownell, Chancellor   *Coast Community College District*
William M. Vega, President   *Coastline Community College*
Leslie N. Purdy, Director   *Office of Alternative Learning Systems*
Mickey Jackson   *Instructional Designer*
Michael S. Werthman   *Publications Editor*
Judith Lindow. McDuff   *Assistant Publications Editor*

Rancho Santiago Community College District

Robert D. Jensen, Chancellor   *Rancho Santiago Community College District*
Richard Sneed, Vice Chancellor of Academic Affairs   *Rancho Santiago Community College District*
Betty Mills, Dean of Instructional Services   *Rancho Santiago College*

Martha L. Lothers, *Illustrations*

The "Designing Home Interiors" telecourse is produced by Coast Community College District and the Rancho Santiago Community College District.

ISBN 0-8087-6937-5

Library of Congress Number Cataloging-in-Publication Data

Hamilton, Judy.
    Designing home interiors.

Rev. ed. of: Designing home interiors / Winifred
Yablonski and Carolyn Breeden. ©1978.
    1. Interior decoration—Study and teaching.
I. Yablonski, Winifred, 1941–   . Designing home
interiors. II. Coast Community College District.
III. Rancho Santiago Community College District.
IV. Title.
NK2116.4.H35   1986   728   86-13682
ISBN 0-8087-6937-5

Printed in the United States of America

H   G   F   E   D   C   B

CONTENTS

PREFACE

TO THE STUDENT

The basic principles of interior design are timeless. Even in the 1980s, when styles seem to change every few months, the generally accepted concepts of visual beauty in our society—of what is pleasing to the eye and spirit—can be traced to esthetic standards established in Greece over two thousand years ago. Likewise, a classical method of inductive reasoning underlies the process of interior design used by both professionals and informed amateurs: gathering information about clients and their needs, preferences, and activities; assembling product and color samples and information; measuring spaces and items of furnishing; and finally arriving at conclusions about the best interior plan for the client.

Because these theories and methods are enduring, quality instructional materials about interior design also endure. The original telecourse, *Designing Home Interiors*, was created in 1978. When the designers and academic consultants began the process of revision in 1986, they found the original course to be amazingly vital.

However, new products and changing life styles did dictate certain revisions in order to make the telecourse relevant to the 1980s and 1990s. The fifth edition of Phyllis Sloan Allen's text, *Beginnings of Interior Environment*, published by Burgess Publishing Company in 1985, covers topics of emerging importance, such as techniques for energy conservation, new fabrics, new lighting systems, floor plans and designs for the single or small-family life style, and the effect of computers on the interior design industry. The new format is not only visually attractive; it also helps students better progress through the learning units and facilitates using the book as a reference. Finally, the text includes the perspective of the professional designer, as well as that of the amateur. All of these new emphases of the text have been incorporated into the telecourse through this revised study guide and through the careful selection and sequencing of the television programs.

Whether you are furnishing your first apartment, purchasing a new home, seeking to more effectively and attractively use existing rooms and furnishings, or considering a career in interior design, we believe that you will find this telecourse rewarding and enriching. Through this course of study, you will become more interested in and sensitive to the concepts of design and will view your surroundings in a more appreciative and critical way. You will also find that you are able to use design methods and principles to create more pleasing and efficient living environments for yourself and for others.

As with most classroom courses, *Designing Home Interiors* has a text, a sequenced plan of study, assignments, and tests. The revised text serves as an ongoing content resource for studying interior design, and this study guide provides a system of study by presenting an overview of each of the twenty-six lessons, reading and viewing assignments, study activities and projects, and study questions. The Student Packet, which accompanies the print materials for this telecourse, is an assortment of activity cards that allow you to practice what you have learned about interior designing, including floor plans, mixing colors, and furniture arrangement. In addition, *Designing Home Interiors* has a special learning component that most classrooms do not have: an opportunity for direct "field" experience through the twenty-six television programs which accompany the study guide lessons. In these programs, you will see hundreds of examples of interior design, meet professional designers and hear them discussing the techniques of their craft, and see graphic demonstrations of concepts such as color and lighting theories, furniture arrangement, and the integration of indoor and outdoor architecture.

The primary academic consultant and writer for this telecourse revision was Judy Hamilton, instructor in the home economics departments of both De Anza and Cañada Community Colleges. Ms. Hamilton received her B.A. in home economics from San Jose State University and has taught courses in interior design, apparel management, clothing construction, fashion, and textiles for over twenty years. She has served as department coordinator for the Los Altos Department of Adult Education, led professional tours of the San Francisco fabric and fashion industries, been a guest lecturer at promotional events for fabric, paint, and wallpaper stores, and consulted as a free-lance home economist for various institutions and industries. In addition, Ms. Hamilton has been course instructor for two telecourses, **Designing Home Interiors** and **Sewing Power**.

Winifred Yablonski and Carolyn Breeden served as academic consultants and coauthored the first edition of this study guide.

COURSE GOALS AND OBJECTIVES

The designers, academic advisers, and producers of **Designing Home Interiors** have established the following course goals and objectives:

Goals

- To provide students with fundamental skills necessary for planning home interiors that are functional, esthetically attractive, and economically feasible.
- To provide consumer information essential to the selection of quality furnishings and materials appropriate for various design plans.
- To demonstrate ways that students can utilize existing furnishings and incorporate them into an overall plan.
- To identify methods used to create a home environment that expresses the personalities of the people within.
- To identify interior design career opportunities and the educational background helpful to those planning to enter this profession.

Objectives

After reading the text assignments, viewing the programs, and completing the assigned study activities and questions, you will be able to:

- Apply the inductive reasoning process in evaluating and planning interior design.
- Define and use the terminology related to interior design.
- Identify and apply the principles and elements of interior design.
- Explain techniques for assessing the quality of home furnishings and accessories.
- Select color combinations and placements which achieve intended effects.

- Given a room of specific dimensions and architectural characteristics, draw a one-fourth-inch-scale floor plan with appropriate architectural and electrical symbols and use furniture templates to create a furnishings, accessories, and lighting arrangement which satisfies the principles of effective design.
- Develop a resource and product information file.
- Create a display board of coordinating furniture and drapery fabrics, carpeting and other flooring, and wall treatment products.
- Explain the responsibilities of and career opportunities for an interior designer.

Specific learning objectives for each of the twenty-six lessons are provided in the chapters of this study guide.

HOW TO TAKE THIS TELECOURSE

If you are new to college courses in general, and television courses in particular, perhaps you can profit from a few suggestions offered by students who have successfully completed other television courses.

Television courses are designed for busy people—people with full-time jobs or family obligations—who want to take a course at home, fitting the study into their personal schedules. In order to take a television course, you will need to plan in advance how to schedule your viewing, reading, study, and design projects. Buy the books before the course begins and look them over, familiarize yourself with any materials supplied by your college, and estimate how much time it will take you to complete special tests and assignments for each lesson. Write the dates of midterms, finals, review sessions, and special projects on your calendar so that you can plan to have extra time to prepare for them. Discuss with your family and friends your needs for study and television viewing time. While you may find it enjoyable and instructive to watch the programs with other people, save the talking and discussion until *after* each program so that you won't miss important information. You may find it helpful to take five minutes at the end of the program to write a brief summary of what you have seen, including the meanings of key terms and concepts.

The study guide will be especially helpful to you as you progress through the course. Begin your study of each lesson by reading the lesson overview, the learning objectives, the assignments for the lesson, and the glossary. Follow the recommended sequence of reading and viewing and then use the study activities to review and study the information in the lesson. As a final step, complete the study questions and check your answers with the answer key at the end of the lesson.

To further ensure that you will complete *Designing Home Interiors* to your satisfaction, you should consider these additional suggestions:

- Buy your own copies of the text and study guide for this course. You will not be able to pass the course without following the assigned exercises in these books.
- Watch all of the television programs. You will need to study both the written and television lessons to complete the tests and assignments.
- Keep up with your work *every week*. Set aside time for reading, viewing, studying, and completing the design projects. Then stick to your schedule.
- Contact the instructor at your college or university if you have questions, need advice or help, or wish to review television programs or watch ones you've missed. More than likely, broadcasts will be repeated at least once by your local station, and video-cassette copies of programs are generally available at your media center or library.

□ Visit furniture stores, design centers or exhibits, and the studios of interior designers whenever possible. Notice the interior environments of your work place, your family, and your friends. Direct observation and analysis will be your most valuable activities in maximizing the benefits of this course.

We hope that you enjoy **Designing Home Interiors** and will come to a deeper appreciation and understanding of the potential for functional and beautiful living and working environments.

Office of Alternative Learning Systems
Coastline Community College

Note Concerning Telecourse Revision

In the first program for this telecourse, instructor Winifred Yablonski shows a copy of the fourth edition of the text and refers to the thirty lessons of the series. We have mentioned that the new fifth edition of the text is now being used with the telecourse. Four of the original telecourse lessons have been eliminated and some of the programs have been resequenced to better coordinate with the sequence of the new text.

WHERE TO BEGIN

OVERVIEW

In the past, the term *interior decorating* was most frequently associated with "beautifying the home." Professionals responsible for this type of work were "interior decorators" whose efforts included the adornment and embellishment of a home environment. By today's standards, interior design involves creating not only an esthetically pleasing environment but also one that is functionally and psychologically acceptable as well as economically feasible. Well-designed interiors are based on the interrelationships of basic structure, furnishings, and environment, with the personalities and life styles of the people who live within. Interiors that are beautiful but fail to satisfy living needs are poorly designed. Equally dissatisfying are extremely functional interiors that project a cold, sterile, impersonal mood and designs that are both functional and beautiful but inappropriate for the family.

Although there are many factors to consider in planning a home environment, the greatest importance should be placed on individual and family **life styles**. This includes such things as the number and ages of people, their resources, values, personalities, tastes, and interpersonal relationships. In other words, how does each person like to live and what are the living patterns of the family as a whole?

Often the most difficult part of interior design can be knowing how or where to begin your project. Lack of information, too much information, too many ideas, or not knowing what to do first can lead to confusion from the start. This lesson suggests background steps considered essential to planning interiors. At this stage, you may not know how to totally evaluate, design, or develop a complete plan, but you can initiate several of the ideas that make interior design work for you. For example, with no knowledge about interior design, you can begin to develop a worthwhile resource file. Then as you work through each lesson, you will acquire the ability to complete the remaining steps in the overall plan.

If there is a cardinal rule in interior design (and this cannot be stressed enough) it is: *Always work with a complete, well thought-out plan.* Whether you are designing a simple storage unit or an entire home, have your ideas firmly in mind and on paper. This provides the opportunity to correct mistakes in the planning process rather than having to live with the frustration of mistakes or the expense of correcting them.

Knowledge and application of basic terminology and design principles are essential to the development and evaluation of your plans. One of the simplest tests to check for a well-designed interior plan is to ask "can it be lived in?" The life styles of the occupants are as important as the appearance and usefulness of any successful plan. Another criterion for evaluation is whether or not the plan allows people to interact with one another in a comfortable manner.

As you view the programs and study the succeeding lessons, you will acquire a basic understanding of interior design guidelines, professional terminology, and artistic design principles that will be helpful to you in developing your own plans. As you learn to work with the principles of design, remember that they should serve as guidelines, not rules.

Throughout this course, keep in mind that a satisfactory interior design plan incorporates **function, economy, beauty,** and **individuality** into a unique whole. You can learn only so much from interior design books. The remainder rests with you. Continued self-education, practice, and experience make the written words come alive.

LEARNING OBJECTIVES

After reading the assignment, viewing the program, and completing the assigned activities, you will be able to accomplish the following objectives:

Comprehension Objectives

1. Define the term "interior design."
2. Discuss the factors to consider in developing an interior design plan that is functionally, psychologically, and economically satisfying.

Skill Objective

1. Develop a resource file of favorite room settings, accessories, and product information for future reference.

ASSIGNMENTS

Before Viewing the Program

- □ Read pages xi–xviii, pages 51–54 in the text, noting particularly those terms listed in the glossary in this lesson.
- □ Read the comprehension and skill objectives for this lesson in the study guide.
- □ Carefully study the overview, highlighting the important points and new concepts.
- □ Look over the study activities and study questions for this lesson.

View the Program "Where to Begin"

While viewing the program, note specifically:

- □ guidelines to be considered when developing a successful interior design plan.
- □ suggestions for developing skills that will enable you to create and evaluate workable interior design plans.

□ how to accumulate and assemble a worthwhile resource file of favorite room settings, accessories, and product information.

After Viewing the Program

□ Review the glossary terms and learning objectives.
□ Complete the study activities.
□ Although Chapters 1 and 2 in your text have no accompanying television programs, it is suggested that you at least scan this material, and it is preferable that you carefully read it. This background information on architectural styles will enhance your appreciation of the fine homes in your community and in other communities you visit. It will also provide an important foundation for your study of interior design.
□ Test your understanding of this lesson by answering the study questions at the end of the lesson. Check your answers with the key.

GLOSSARY

(Page numbers refer to your text.)

beauty, page 53

economy, page 51

function, page 51

individuality, page 54

interior designer: a professional who creates environmental plans for home or business that are psychologically sound, esthetically pleasing, functional, and economically feasible for the client.

life style: the activities, interests, tastes, personalities, values, and resources of an individual or family.

STUDY ACTIVITIES

Required Activities

1. Devise an organized system for filing interior design ideas and articles you collect.
2. Using your newspapers, advertising supplements, local magazines, and telephone directory, make a list of at least ten resources of design ideas available to you.
3. Choose one of the following activities and write a two-page paper describing your findings or ideas.
   □ Begin listing comments about how your family lives, its activities, habits, and preferences. Keep reviewing and adding to the list for several days. When the list appears complete, draw conclusions about the life styles expressed within your family and how the interior environment should function to satisfy your needs.
   □ List and consider at least five factors that would influence your interior design plans. Briefly explain the relationship of each factor to your design decisions.
   □ Analyze the relationship of function, economy, beauty, and individuality to a well-designed interior plan.

Extra-Credit Activities

The following activities are based on Chapters 1 and 2 in your text.

1. Many institutions offering this telecourse will be supplied with a set of slides which give further visual examples of the concepts introduced in your text. Contact your instructor to see if these slides are available and, if they are, arrange to view the architectural examples accompanying Lessons One and Two. Be sure to read the booklet that provides descriptions of and information about these slides. Write a two-page paper describing what you learned from this viewing.

2. Find a home in your community or a neighboring one that is at least seventy-five years old. Visit the home and try to identify its architectural style, supporting your identification with exterior design details which are like those you studied in your text. Write a two-page paper describing the house and your conclusions about its style. If possible, supply a picture of the home with your report.

STUDY QUESTIONS

(Select the one best answer.)

Comprehension Objective 1:   Define the term "interior design."

1. The main function of an interior designer is best described as
   a. decorating a home.
   b. arranging furnishings.
   c. coordinating interior colors.
   d. creating a functional, attractive, psychologically sound environment.

2. The simplest test to check whether a room is well-designed is to ask
   a. is it affordable?
   b. are the colors pleasing?
   c. can it be lived in?
   d. does it "feel" good to be in the room?

Comprehension Objective 2:   Discuss the factors to consider in developing a plan that is functionally, psychologically, and economically satisfying.

3. The advantage(s) of working with a complete, well thought-out plan is (are)
   a. buying everything at once often entitles you to discount prices.
   b. it is easier to prevent costly mistakes.
   c. having a plan guarantees your success.
   d. described by all of the above statements.

4. Which of the following factors are the most important considerations of a well-designed interior plan?
   a. the age of a house and its geographic location
   b. function, beauty, economy, individuality
   c. color, balance, texture
   d. paint, wallpaper, wood fixtures, carpeting

5. Which of the following is the *most* important function of a home?
   a. satisfying the needs of the people who live there
   b. having a well-planned traffic pattern
   c. being esthetically pleasing
   d. having well-designed plumbing, water, and heating systems

6. A person who is building a home can best limit costs by
   a. working with a reputable architect.
   b. beginning with a good design.
   c. avoiding unnecessary mixing of materials.
   d. doing all of the above.
   e. taking the actions described in b and c.

7. It is cheaper in the long run to have professionals do the finish work, such as painting or laying flooring, on a home.
   a. true
   b. false

ANSWER KEY

(Page numbers refer to your text.)

1. d (study guide, television program)
2. c (study guide)
3. b (study guide, television program)
4. b (study guide, pages 51–54)
5. a (page 51)
6. e (page 52)
7. b (page 53)

LESSON
2

DOLLARS AND SENSE

OVERVIEW

Successfully designed interiors don't just happen. And no amount of luck or sheer magic will camouflage or compensate for the lack of good planning. In Lesson One, "Where to Begin," you learned that the development of a complete interior plan is one of the essential steps in making interior design work for you. Without such a plan, failure is almost a guarantee. Although creating a plan cannot insure total success, it will certainly provide less chance for error and give you the opportunity to visualize the end result before spending any money.

The television program shows how one couple handled the problem of creating a more livable environment for their son by following sequential guidelines to develop a workable plan. When you begin applying these guidelines to your own situation you may think of one or two additional steps you would like to include, or perhaps you may choose a slightly different sequence. Note, however, it is important not to omit any of the steps and to plan a logical sequence. For example, if a room is to function well and satisfy the needs of the individuals who use it, life styles must be identified before planning a furniture arrangement.

Below is a review of the sequence of specific steps for **interior-plan development** as presented in the television program:

Steps in Plan Development

1. Identify life styles.
2. Determine needs and wants in relation to life styles.
3. Know your resources—human, financial, and material.
4. Establish the theme or mood desired.
5. Complete a floor plan evaluation.
6. Complete a one-fourth-inch scale drawing of the floor plan.
7. Plan the furniture arrangement by using furniture templates. Add built-in structures to the plan by using templates on a wall as well as a floor scale drawing.
8. Select samples for structural and portable furnishings.
9. Visualize and evaluate the samples in relation to life styles, theme or mood desired, and design principles.
10. Evaluate the total plan in relation to present resources.
11. Revise the plan as needed.

Although it is important to outline sequential steps for creating an interior design plan, keep in mind that initially you are developing only a broad concept, and the specific details can be decided upon later. Future lessons will focus on specific areas, such as developing floor plans, selecting colors and fabrics, creating a mood, and coordinating furnishings while applying the basic design principles.

Financial planning is another important consideration. One of the best ways to help you identify how much you might be able to spend on furnishings is to evaluate your income or the price of your dwelling in relation to percentages suggested by financial institutions. Remember these are only guidelines and should be analyzed with respect to your own situation and values.

The first expenditure plan, which includes projections for furnishings as well as major appliances, states that you should expect eventually to spend 25 to 33 percent of one year's gross income to complete an interior design plan. A second plan suggests that you estimate 25 to 33 percent of the dwelling's price as a base to be spent for furnishings. The figures obtained by these two methods may be vastly different, due to the tremendous increase in the cost of homes during the past few years. Whether furnishing a home or a rental dwelling, it may be safer and more realistic to base your furnishings budget on income rather than the price of the dwelling.

After you know about how much you will spend for your furnishings, determine a period of time in which you feel you could reasonably handle the expenditures. It is not unusual to consider a three-to-five-year financial plan for completing the design of a larger dwelling. Also, if you prefer to spend a larger amount than suggested by the guidelines, you may find it necessary to divide the expenditures over a longer period.

When you do begin to purchase furnishings, think through the various ways you can pay for the products, and evaluate the payment methods to determine which ones suit you. In addition to paying cash for some products, you may want to purchase others on **credit**. The ninety-day plan is one form of credit purchasing that usually does not include a finance charge. Revolving charge accounts, loans from credit unions, banks, or financial companies, and credit extended by retail stores involve interest charges, and you should fully understand and calculate these charges prior to signing the **credit contract**. It is possible and acceptable to "shop" for credit by comparing the **annual percentage rates** charged by the various companies. Because the annual rates can vary from approximately 9 percent to 30 percent, you can save substantial amounts of money by taking the time to shop for credit. Most consumers find that a combination of payment methods is most satisfactory.

Budgeting for furnishings is one of the most important aspects of successful interior designing. Few things can so quickly destroy your enthusiasm and your plans as overextending your budget. Therefore, recognize the importance of evaluating your design ideas in relation to your financial scheme and know how to make the best use of your money or credit when it is time to purchase the furnishings.

LEARNING OBJECTIVES

After reading the assignment, viewing the program, and completing the assigned activities, you will be able to accomplish the following objectives:

Comprehension Objectives

1. Explain the importance of developing a complete interior plan prior to making initial or additional purchases.

2. Identify the consumer guidelines for establishing the financial resources available when implementing a design plan.
3. Compare and contrast three methods of financing a design plan, noting the positive and negative features of each method.

Skill Objective

1. Design a sequential pattern of essential steps for developing an interior plan.

ASSIGNMENTS

Before Viewing the Program

- Read the comprehension and skill objectives for this lesson in the study guide.
- Carefully study the overview, highlighting the important points and new concepts.
- Look after the glossary terms, study activities, and study questions for this lesson.

View the Program, "Dollars and Sense"

While viewing the program, note specifically:

- the steps in developing a sequential interior design plan.
- how to determine the financial resources available for implementing a design plan.
- various means of financing the purchase of home furnishings available to consumers and the advantages of each.
- the disadvantage of paying cash at the time furnishings are delivered.

After Viewing the Program

- Review the glossary terms and learning objectives.
- Complete the study activities.
- Test your understanding of this lesson by answering the study questions at the end of the lesson. Check your answers with the key.

GLOSSARY

annual percentage rate: the total yearly percentage rate paid as interest on money borrowed to finance major purchases.

credit: a way of purchasing furnishings by means of deferred or delayed payment, thus allowing time for a more careful evaluation of purchases.

credit contract: a legal document outlining the manner in which payment will be made for items purchased. This document may be a simple ninety-day contract with no interest charges or a two-to-five-year contract with finance charges.

furnishing expenditure guidelines: budgetary guidelines which suggest the percentage of annual income to be spent on furnishings. The value of the dwelling also serves as a guideline; in both cases the standard recommended amount should not exceed 25 to 33 percent of the yearly gross income or of the value of the house.

sequential interior-plan development: a logical, step-by-step plan for creating a workable interior design plan.

STUDY ACTIVITIES

Required Activities

1. Prepare a sequential list of the essential steps in developing an interior plan. Explain how the sequence can be varied to meet individual needs.
2. Choose two of the following activities and write a one-to-two-page paper with your answers or comments.
   - Discuss the advantages of developing an interior-design plan before you purchase furnishings.
   - Describe what is meant by sequential interior planning.
   - Discuss the primary disadvantage of paying cash for furnishings.
   - Define the ninety-day payment plan. Explain the advantages of this method of payment.
   - Describe how a knowledgeable consumer will shop for credit.

STUDY QUESTIONS

(Select the one best answer.)

Comprehension Objective 1:   Explain the importance of developing a complete interior plan prior to making initial or additional purchases.

1. The chief advantage(s) of having a workable, well thought-out interior plan is (are)
   a. it will keep you from spending more than you have.
   b. you can shop around at different stores for the best prices.
   c. it is easier to prevent costly mistakes.
   d. described by all of the above statements.

   Identify the proper sequence for developing an interior design plan by lettering the following steps as "a" for the first step, "b" for the second, "c" for the third, and "d" for the final step.

   _____ 2. evaluate floor plan
   _____ 3. determine needs and wants
   _____ 4. identify life styles
   _____ 5. select fabrics, furnishings, and color scheme

Comprehension Objective 2:   Identify the consumer guidelines for establishing the financial resources available when implementing a design plan.

6. The suggested percentage of gross annual income which should be planned for expenditure on interior furnishings is
   a. 10 to 20 percent.
   b. 25 to 33 percent.
   c. 30 to 40 percent.
   d. 50 percent the first year, less in subsequent years.

7. A family who wishes to spend more on furnishings than the consumer guidelines suggest should
   a. plan their purchases in stages which span several years.
   b. reconsider and modify their desires and tastes.
   c. arrange long-term financing for their purchases.
   d. reduce their expenditures in other areas of their budget.

Comprehension Objective 3: Compare and contrast three methods of financing a design plan, noting the positive and negative features of each method.

8. Which of the following furnishings payment methods is (are) the most financially advantageous?
   a. cash
   b. long-term (one year or more) credit
   c. ninety-day credit
   d. cash or ninety-day credit
   e. either cash or long-term credit

9. A primary disadvantage of paying cash at the time of delivery is that
   a. financial resources are depleted all at once.
   b. it is just as cheap to arrange ninety-day credit.
   c. the customer has no financial leverage if the furnishings prove unsatisfactory.
   d. most families are more comfortable with small monthly cash outlays than large single ones.

10. An important part of evaluating a time payment contract is considering the
    a. annual percentage rate.
    b. monthly percentage rate.
    c. default penalty.
    d. factors described in a and c.

ANSWER KEY

1. c (television program)
2. c (television program)
3. b (television program)
4. a (television program)
5. d (television program)

6. b (study guide, television program)
7. a (television program)
8. d (study guide)
9. c (television program)
10. d (television program)

DESIGN BASICS

OVERVIEW

Design is everywhere around you, in the natural world as well as the world created by humans. What you see, touch, and work with on a daily basis are examples of design and are composed of **line, form or mass, space, color,** and **texture—the elements of design.** Lesson Three focuses on understanding how these elements work together to create the attractive, well-designed components of an interior design plan.

To better understand how these components work together, closely examine any object in your immediate surrounds; for example, a chair, table, or lamp. The lines of this object join together to create its form or mass. It is surrounded by space, defined as **negative space,** but it also occupies a specific area called **positive space.** Color and texture enhance its beauty and capture our attention.

Our goal in studying interior design is to become consciously more aware of design. As your text states, the best way to learn to recognize the difference between good and bad design is to develop the habit of keen observation. Learn to see how various elements interrelate to produce a design; *look* at objects and become familiar with the use of line, form or mass, space, color, and texture. If you become perceptive and acquire the ability to observe, study, experiment, and analyze in this way, you will develop a sense of what constitutes good design.

Just as there is no universal concept of beauty, neither are there any rigid rules that clearly delineate good design. Therefore, keep in mind that learning interior design is not a matter of accepting standards set by others. It is a process of becoming more perceptive and developing your ability to use design elements. Rather than memorize rules, develop an appreciation of what factors have been proven successful in good design.

To understand design you must be familiar with the two broad categories of design— **structural** and applied **decorative design.** Structural design has little if any applied ornament. The structure itself determines the form of the design, and enrichment comes from the materials used. Decorative design relies on applied line, texture, or color to enhance the basic structure. In order to be esthetically pleasing, any applied design should be in harmony with the shape and function of the structure.

Everyone has his or her personal preferences, or what is sometimes called "personal taste." Even though we all feel that our personal choices reflect **good taste,** we still must be aware that our preferences may not always be an accurate assessment of good design. Learn to recognize good design in rooms, furniture, and various objects, even if they do not express your own taste. Probably, in the process of developing an appreciation of good design, you will find your own personal preferences changing, evolving, and growing.

As you view the program, be aware of the methods and criteria used to analyze and evaluate home furnishings and room settings. Observe how the elements—line, form or mass, space, and texture—interrelate to create a total composition or complete design. Note that the creative and effective use of the elements of design can make it possible to camouflage or correct undesirable effects in an overall design. Small areas can be made to appear larger, while vast areas can be made to feel more intimate. Once you have acquired an understanding of the design elements, you will find it easier to tailor visual space to your needs.

LEARNING OBJECTIVES

After reading the assignment, viewing the program, and completing the assigned activities, you will be able to accomplish the following objectives:

Comprehension Objectives

1. Explain the importance of the design elements (line, form or mass, space, texture, and color) as they relate to an interior plan.
2. Discuss the problems of defining good taste.
3. Define and cite examples of structural and decorative design.

Skill Objectives

1. Given one picture of a room setting, identify the elements of design. Analyze the relationships of form or mass, space, line, color, and texture to the overall design.
2. Identify examples of naturalistic, stylized, geometric, and abstract designs.

ASSIGNMENTS

Before Viewing the Program

- Read pages 65–77 in the text, noting particularly those terms listed in the glossary in this lesson.
- Read the comprehension and skill objectives for this lesson in the study guide.
- Carefully study the overview, highlighting the important points and new concepts.
- Look over the study activities and study questions for this lesson.

View the Program "Design Basics"

While viewing the program, note specifically:

- examples of line, form or mass, space, texture, and color and how these elements of design can be used to create specific effects.

□ how the elements of design are interrelated and can vary the total effect of a room.

□ examples of and the difference between structural and applied design as discussed by Ms. Yablonski and the guest designer, Robert Thorpe.

□ the characteristics of these decorative design classifications: naturalistic, stylized, geometric, and abstract.

□ the discussion of personal performance or taste.

After Viewing the Program

□ Review the glossary terms and learning objectives.

□ Complete the study activities.

□ Test your understanding of this lesson by answering the study questions at the end of the lesson. Check your answers with the key.

GLOSSARY

(Page numbers refer to your text.)

decorative design, page 69

elements of design, page 70

form or mass, page 77

good taste, page 67

line, page 73

negative space: the blank or empty space surrounding an object or mass.

pattern, page 73

positive space: the specific area an object occupies.

structural design, page 68

texture, page 70

STUDY ACTIVITIES

Required Activities

1. Select a picture of a furnished room that you feel represents good structural and decorative design. Write a one-to-two-page paper, evaluating and discussing the designs according to the composition of the elements and the criteria established in your text and the program.

2. Examine Figures 5.1, 5.15, 6.1, 6.7, 6.8, 6.9, and 6.10 of your text and label the patterns shown in floor, wall, window, and furniture coverings according to the following classifications of decorative design: naturalistic, stylized, geometric, and abstract.

Extra-Credit Activity

1. Find two examples of how lines can focus attention and create optical illusions. Describe the examples in a one-to-two-page paper, attaching appropriate pictures if they are available.

STUDY QUESTIONS

(Select the one best answer.)

Comprehension Objective 1:   Explain the importance of the design elements (line, form or mass, space, texture, and color) as they relate to an interior plan.

1. Which of the following groups of categories best describes the design element "line"?
   a. left, right, up, down
   b. north, south, east, west
   c. vertical, horizontal, diagonal, curved
   d. rectangle, square, circle, triangle
2. Which of the following relates to texture as a design element?
   a. roughness and smoothness
   b. soft or hard surfaces
   c. shiny or dull surfaces
   d. all of the above
3. Positive space refers to
   a. a nice place to work.
   b. the specific area an object occupies.
   c. space having a dual purpose.
   d. the area surrounding an object or furnishing.

Match the descriptive statements on the left with the design elements on the right by writing the corresponding letters in the blanks provided. Answers can be used more than once.

_____ 4. establishes the formality of a room	a. line
_____ 5. can be used to establish a feeling of motion or repose	b. texture
	c. color
_____ 6. the most important, and least costly, element of design	d. form or mass
_____ 7. is both visual and tactile	
_____ 8. affects the illusion of size of a room	

Comprehension Objective 2:   Discuss the problems of defining good taste.

9. A novice interior designer can begin developing a sense of "good taste" by
   a. studying the elements of design.
   b. learning to recognize good design.
   c. becoming more observant of design details.
   d. doing all of the above.
10. Good taste is a discriminating quality that can be achieved quickly by familiarizing yourself with high-quality, expensive furnishings.
    a. true
    b. false

Comprehension Objective 3:   Define and cite examples of structural and decorative design.

11. Which of the following attributes is *not* essential to successful structural design?
    a. simplicity
    b. good proportion
    c. appropriateness of materials
    d. suitability
    e. placement

12. Decorative design falls into four classifications:
    a. stripes, plaids, zigzags, diagonals.
    b. conventional, contemporary, futuristic, historic.
    c. naturalistic, stylized, geometric, abstract.
    d. walls, window coverings, floors, ceilings.

Identify the following design examples as (a) structural or (b) decorative.

_____ 13. wallpaper with a geometric pattern
_____ 14. a square, glass-topped coffee table with a square wooden base
_____ 15. a sofa covered in a flowered fabric
_____ 16. a lamp with a curved wooden base and pleated shade

ANSWER KEY

(Page numbers refer to your text.)

1. c (pages 73–77)
2. d (pages 70–72)
3. b (study guide, television program)
4. b (pages 70–72, television program)
5. a (pages 73–77, television program)
6. c (page 77, television program)
7. b (pages 70–72, television program)
8. d (page 77, television program)
9. d (study guide, television program)
10. b (page 67)
11. e (page 68)
12. c (page 69, television program)
13. b (pages 68–70)
14. a (pages 68–70)
15. b (pages 68–70)
16. b (pages 68–70)

PRINCIPLES OF DESIGN

OVERVIEW

Interior design should be based on the selection and arrangement of the design elements (line, form or mass, space, color, and texture) according to the **principles of design**. The principles of design—proportion, scale, balance, rhythm, emphasis, and harmony—are used to create an orderly and pleasing interior arrangement. To be able to differentiate between good and poor design, you must know and understand these six principles. The program for this lesson closely examines five of the six design principles and illustrates how to successfully evaluate and apply these principles.

The formulation of these principles is not a new aspect of interior design but has evolved from centuries of study and observation. The pleasing visual elements of nature and great works of art have been important resources for this study.

Proportion is defined as the relation of one part to another or to the whole, or of one object to another. Although no foolproof system of proportioning has been devised that holds true in every situation, the ancient Greeks developed three theories to identify and establish pleasing proportions. They have been identified as the **golden mean**, the **golden rectangle**, and the **golden section**; and these theories are well illustrated on page 79 of your text. The basic premise of all three theories is that unequal proportion is more interesting and pleasing than areas divided into equal portions.

Scale refers primarily to the size of objects in relation to other objects and to people. Scale is usually referred to as either large or small, depending on the point of comparison. Good scale is the result of a pleasing relationship of all components in a space. When selecting and organizing furnishings for an interior space, make sure that they are scaled to people, to each other, and to the space in which they will be used.

Balance in interior design is equilibrium as the eye perceives it. You will need to become familiar with the psychological effect of "visual balance" because objects tend to appear equalized in a space. When a room is well balanced, things look as if they belong where they are; it is a comfortable setting. Balance can be divided into three types: **formal**, **informal**, and **radial**. In formal balance, one side of an arrangement is the mirror image of the other. Equilibrium is easily achieved through the application of formal balance, as you will observe in many traditionally planned interiors. Informal balance is, perhaps, more difficult to achieve because there is no set formula for creating it. However, with a little imagination and creative arrangement, you can make the components of a design appear to have equal weight even though they are different. Radial balance results when there is circular movement from or toward a central point.

Rhythm is the intangible element of composition that keeps the eye traveling from one part of an arrangement to another. This can be achieved through **gradation**, **repetition**, **opposition**, **transition**, and **radiation**. Your text gives simple but effective illustrations by creating rhythm on page 82. Study these and you will better understand how rhythm makes designs come alive through implied movement and direction.

The focal point or center of interest in a room illustrates the principle of **emphasis**. Any successful design must have a dominant feature to which all other aspects lend their support. A fireplace or bay window are examples of dominant architectural features that can easily be developed into the center of emphasis. Lacking architectural features, color, lighting, and decorative accessories can be implemented to create emphasis. When creating a pattern of emphasis, decide how important each unit should be and then give it the proper amount of visual importance.

When the design principles of balance, scale, proportion, rhythm, and emphasis are effectively applied **harmony** is the result. You will learn about harmony in the next lesson.

LEARNING OBJECTIVES

After reading the assignment, viewing the program, and completing the assigned activities, you will be able to accomplish the following objectives:

Comprehension Objectives

1. Define the following principles of design: proportion, scale, balance, rhythm, emphasis, and harmony.
2. Explain the visual difference between formal and informal balance.
3. Identify three possible ways to achieve a major point of emphasis within a room.
4. Explain how rhythm can be created in a design plan.

Skill Objectives

1. Given two pictures of chairs, select a correctly scaled table and lamp for each.
2. Given linear wall space, select a correctly proportioned sofa length for that space.
3. Evaluate one picture of a room setting according to the following principles of design: proportion, scale, balance, rhythm, and emphasis.

ASSIGNMENTS

Before Viewing the Program

- Read pages 77–83 in the text, noting particularly those terms listed in the glossary in this lesson.
- Read the comprehension and skill objectives for this lesson in the study guide.

□ Carefully study the overview, highlighting the important points and new concepts.
□ Look over the study activities and study questions for this lesson.

View the Program "Principles of Design"

While viewing the program, note specifically:

□ how the elements of design differ from the design principles. Notice what factors comprise each category.
□ visual examples of the first five principles of design.
□ the difference between formal and informal balance.
□ the factors which combine to create rhythm in an interior design.
□ how dominant and subordinate factors relate to emphasis.
□ the artists—Ann, Don, Pete, and Tom—correcting design problems with room sketches.
□ interior designer Carole Eichen analyzing design principles as they are applied in furnishing a model home.

After Viewing the Program

□ Review the glossary terms and learning objectives.
□ Complete the study activities.
□ Test your understanding of this lesson by answering the study questions at the end of the lesson. Check your answers with the key.

GLOSSARY

(Page numbers refer to your text.)
balance, page 80
emphasis, page 82
formal balance, page 80
golden mean, page 79
golden rectangle, page 79
golden section, page 79
gradation, page 82
informal balance, page 80
opposition, page 82
principles of design, page 77
proportion, page 78
radial balance, page 80
radiation, page 82
repetition, page 82
rhythm, page 82
scale, page 78
transition, page 82

STUDY ACTIVITIES

Required Activities

1. Using plate 12 in the student packet as your floor plan and template 1 for the furnishings, plan two functional furniture arrangements, one representing formal balance, one informal balance.
2. Study Figure 4.11 in your text. Evaluate the design in terms of how the six principles of design are applied and write a one-to-two-page paper describing your evaluation.

Extra-Credit Activities

1. Evaluate one of your own rooms according to the principles of design. Write a one-to-two-page paper describing your evaluation and identifying possible changes that would improve the room's design.
2. Using graph paper, make a simple wall drawing that includes two chairs, a table with a lamp, and pictures behind the chairs. Make the furnishings fit proportions of a wall space that is nine feet wide by eight feet high. Using the "golden mean" found in your text, calculate the proportions and then arrange the furniture accordingly. Refer to page 78 of your text when necessary.

STUDY QUESTIONS

(Select the one best answer.)

Comprehension Objective 1:   Define the following principles of design: proportion, scale, balance, rhythm, emphasis, and harmony.

Match the terms on the left which best relate to the principles of design on the right by writing the corresponding letters in the blanks provided.

_____ 1. center of interest	a.	proportion
_____ 2. formal and informal	b.	scale
_____ 3. compares overall size	c.	balance
_____ 4. utilizes the "golden section" theory	d.	rhythm
_____ 5. unifies all the elements	e.	emphasis
_____ 6. gives a smooth visual transition from one area to another	f.	harmony

Comprehension Objective 2:   Explain the visual difference between formal and informal balance.

7. Formal balance in a room could be best described as
   a. furnishings featuring marble, tapestries, and Persian rugs.
   b. a casual grouping of many different pieces of furniture.
   c. upholstery fabrics and wall coverings that match.
   d. an arrangement in which one-half of an area is a mirror image of the other half.

8. Which of the following is (are) the most interesting and long-lasting type(s) of balance?
   a. bisymmetrical
   b. asymmetrical
   c. radial
   d. either bisymmetrical or radial

Comprehension Objective 3:   Identify three possible ways to achieve a major point of emphasis in a room.

9. In the absence of a dominant architectural feature, which of the following would be most useful in developing or enhancing a point of interest in a room?
   a. plants, decorative screens, mirrors
   b. color, lighting, accessories
   c. paint, wallpaper, carpeting
   d. draperies, upholstery fabrics, carpeting

10. A single decorative piece of art, such as a mural, painting, weaving, or rug, can be used as a dominant feature when creating a focal point.
    a. true
    b. false

11. How should the furniture arrangement relate to the point of emphasis in a room?
    a. The point of emphasis should be clear of furnishings so that it is more noticeable.
    b. Other furnishings should balance the point of emphasis in scale and proportion.
    c. Comfortable furniture should be grouped around the point of emphasis.
    d. The guidelines described in b and c should be observed.

Comprehension Objective 4:   Explain how rhythm can be created in a design plan.
   Match the descriptions on the left with the methods used to create rhythm in interior design on the right by writing the corresponding letters in the blanks provided.

_____ 12. use of curved line to lead the eye, such as with arched windows or drapery swags	a. repetition
	b. gradation
	c. opposition
_____ 13. lines extending out from a central point	d. transition
	e. radiation
_____ 14. lines converging at right angles	
_____ 15. objects increasing in size—small, to medium, to large	
_____ 16. recurring use of color, pattern, line, texture, or form	

ANSWER KEY

(Page numbers refer to your text.)

1. e (page 82, television program)
2. c (pages 80–81, television program)
3. b (pages 78–80, television program)
4. a (pages 78–80, television program)
5. f (page 83)
6. d (page 82, television program)
7. d (page 80, study guide)
8. b (page 80, television program, study guide)

9. b (page 82)
10. a (page 82)
11. b (page 82)
12. d (page 82, television program)
13. e (page 82)
14. c (page 82)
15. b (page 82)
16. a (page 82)

THEMES AND MOODS

OVERVIEW

Have you ever walked into a room and felt that all its components work together? This unified feeling doesn't just happen. It results only when the room's entire design expresses all the principles of design.

Lesson Four, "Principles of Design," concentrated on five of the basic principles of design: proportion, scale, balance, rhythm, and emphasis. When these five have been successfully interrelated in one design, the last basic principle, **harmony**, is achieved.

Harmonious rooms are based on a single theme, or mood, and the basic categories for the theme of a room are formal and informal. The **degree of formality**, however, can vary, from the most elegantly formal to an extremely informal, rustic mood. In the television program for this lesson you will see rooms with five different moods, each expressing a different degree of formality.

In addition to these two basic categories of theme and the degrees between the categories, mood can also be described by such terms as warm, casual, tranquil, invigorating, cool, and luxurious. Whatever the category or description, a harmonious room strikes the eye as unified, with each element contributing to the designer's overall thematic intent.

Rooms that have this harmonious relationship may not reflect your personal taste, but you will generally find that the design is interesting and pleasing. The next time you view a room setting that you find attractive, try to determine why you feel the room is well designed. Most often, your eye will focus first on the major point of emphasis in the room and rhythmically travel to the other, less dominant, segments. The room will appear visually balanced, and all components will be in proportion to one another and to the room as a whole. The room and all its furnishings express a unified, harmonious theme because of the use and application of the design elements and principles.

In a harmonious design plan, it is important to consider the role each design principle plays. Balance, scale, proportion, emphasis, and rhythm must be considered separately and then in relation to one another.

While following these basic guidelines assures a harmonious design, it is important to avoid monotony by planning a degree of variety. For example, a room that has only one specific fabric texture would be plain and uninteresting because it would lack the balance of unity with variety.

Therefore, try to "fine-tune" your senses so that you will recognize when a room has sufficient unity to be harmonious but also includes the variety necessary for interest.

One of the easiest ways to begin planning the design for a room is to select a **theme** or mood that will be compatible with your life style or one that reflects your interests. As you proceed with the selection of furnishings to carry out that theme, apply a basic rule to evaluate the appropriateness of an item. Question whether the item is useful, beautiful, or meaningful to the people using it.

LEARNING OBJECTIVES

After reading the assignment, viewing the program, and completing the assigned activities, you will be able to accomplish the following objectives:

Comprehension Objectives

1. Explain the process of developing a mood or theme in an interior design plan.
2. Relate the principles and elements of design to the development of an effective interior plan.

Skill Objectives

1. Analyze two room settings according to the elements and principles of design used and list changes that would improve the total design.
2. Identify two different themes for a specific room and explain how to apply the elements and principles of design to achieve each theme.

ASSIGNMENTS

Before Viewing the Program

□ Review pages 77–83 in the text, noting particularly those terms listed in the glossary in this lesson.
□ Read the comprehension and skill objectives for this lesson in the study guide.
□ Carefully study the overview, highlighting the important points and new concepts.
□ Look over the study activities and study questions for this lesson.

View the Program "Themes and Moods"

While viewing the program, note specifically:

□ Ms. Yablonski's review of the principles of design—balance, scale, proportion, emphasis, and rhythm—and how these principles work together, creating a unifying sense of order known as harmony.
□ the varying degrees of formality and informality possible in a home environment.
□ the terminology that can be used to describe the mood, look, feeling, or theme of a room or home.
□ how furnishings and accessories can be grouped to reflect a unified theme or mood.

After Viewing the Program

- ☐ Review the glossary terms and learning objectives.
- ☐ Complete the study activities.
- ☐ Test your understanding of this lesson by answering the study questions at the end of the lesson. Check your answers with the key.

GLOSSARY

(Page numbers refer to your text.)

degree of formality, page 83

harmony, page 83

theme: the conscious reflection of an attitude, mood, interest, or feeling in a well-designed room. Usually represented by furniture, color, fabric, floor coverings, and accessories.

unity with variety: the harmonious blending of the principles of design with enough variation of color, pattern, and texture to be interesting.

STUDY ACTIVITIES

Required Activities

1. Complete the assignment on page 98 in your text.
2. Identify a theme for an imaginary room and select or describe a fabric, a floor covering, a wall covering, and one accessory expressing that theme.

Extra-Credit Activities

1. Select a furnished room in a model home or in a retail store and write a two-to-three-page paper analyzing the room according to the principles of design. Identify possible changes that could improve the designs.
2. Study the individual rooms in your home and determine if each expresses a single theme. List and describe the factors of each room which either enhance or distract from its design unity.
3. Select a patterned fabric or wallpaper and write a one-to-two page paper explaining how the principles of design have or have not been applied.

STUDY QUESTIONS

(Select the one best answer.)

Comprehension Objective 1:   Explain the process of developing a mood or theme in an interior design plan.

1. When developing a theme for a room, the dominant feature would represent which of the following principles of design?
   a. proportion
   b. balance
   c. scale
   d. emphasis

2. The "common denominator" of a room plan is also referred to as
   a. the color scheme.
   b. consistently using the same period of furniture.
   c. a unifying theme.
   d. repetition.

3. To create a formal, eighteenth-century French theme in a room, which of the following components is *inappropriate*?
   a. soft pastel colors
   b. silk damask fabrics
   c. Persian rugs
   d. homespun fabrics

Comprehension Objective 2:   Relate the principles and elements of design to the development of an effective interior plan.

Match the principles and the elements of design on the right with the appropriate descriptions on the left by writing the corresponding letters in the blanks provided.

_____ 4. the contour of an object as represented by its shape

_____ 5. the most important, yet least costly, design component

_____ 6. the surface quality of an object; greatly variable

_____ 7. that which deserves or demands the most attention in a room

_____ 8. when traveling in a specific direction, an element which can inspire a feeling of motion or repose

_____ 9. an element which applies Greek theories for best results

_____ 10. the quality described as being asymmetrical, bisymmetrical, or radial

_____ 11. a flowing quality which often guides the eye from place to place

_____ 12. surface enrichment or embellishment

_____ 13. the result when all the principles of design work together effectively

_____ 14. an element which, when well planned and well organized, produces a feeling of tranquility

_____ 15. an illuminating feature appearing in many forms

a. color
b. emphasis
c. line
d. proportion
e. space
f. balance
g. texture
h. unity or harmony
i. pattern
j. form or mass
k. light
l. rhythm

ANSWER KEY

(Page numbers refer to your text.)

1. d (page 82)
2. c (study guide, page 83)
3. d (page 83)
4. j (page 77)
5. a (page 77)
6. g (page 70)
7. b (page 82)
8. c (page 73)

9. d (page 78)
10. f (page 80)
11. l (page 82)
12. i (page 72)
13. h (page 83)
14. e (page 77)
15. k (page 77)

MAPPING
IT OUT

OVERVIEW

Developing a functional and attractive room plan involves more than creating a mental picture of how to arrange the furnishings. Often, however, developing a mental plan is the first step many people take when furnishing and designing their homes. A wiser approach is presented in the television program for this lesson, "Mapping It Out," which outlines important preliminary steps on how to draw floor plans that will be helpful in achieving a functional and attractive interior design.

A major benefit of planning on paper is determining the exact furniture sizes needed. Impulse buying and other costly mistakes can be more easily curtailed when a definite plan is followed. Additionally, if you expect to employ craftsmen to complete some of the interior work, these plans can help the workers more accurately understand your exact needs.

Finally, planning on paper provides an excellent opportunity to double-check your design ideas against the functional needs determined for the room. Traffic patterns can be evaluated and deficiencies corrected before you begin implementing the plan.

As you begin the actual design process for your home, your first step should be to complete a one-fourth-inch scale drawing of the floor plan for each room you plan to furnish. The basic equipment includes a drawing board, one-fourth-inch grid graph paper, pencils, felt pens, ruler or architectural scale, masking tape, one-eighth-inch wide pressure sensitive tape (for indicating walls), an eraser, a mat knife, and a compass. Although not all of these items are absolutely essential they will help you complete the work as quickly and accurately as possible. For example, you may draw your plan on plain paper, but scale conversion is easier when using one-fourth-inch grid graph paper. (Note that this paper can be found in the student packet.)

Your initial sketch of a room need not be to scale, but the essential measurements should be accurately recorded on the sketch. Then, as you begin your scale drawings, mark the exact positions of all architectural features, doors, windows, the fireplace, closets, and electrical details such as fixtures, switches, and electrical outlets. An example of a scale-drawn floor plan with furnishings in place is shown on page 270 of your text. You'll also learn in this lesson how to apply scale-drawing techniques when making elevation drawings of specific walls. Although scaled elevation drawings are not necessary at this time, knowing how to use this information will be helpful in future lessons.

When the scale drawing for each room is completed, use furniture templates, or small patterns of the furniture pieces, to try out your ideas for furniture arrangements and additional built-ins before you actually begin purchasing. (Several sets of templates can be found in the student packet. Also, standard templates are available at stationery and artist supplies stores.) Templates will be more accurate than either a tape measure or guesswork in giving you a picture of how various pieces will work in the room. The entire family can participate in these planning stages before the final decisions are made.

LEARNING OBJECTIVES

After reading the assignment, viewing the program, and completing the assigned activities, you will be able to accomplish the following objectives:

Comprehension Objectives

1. Identify and accurately describe all architectural and electrical symbols used to draw a scale floor plan for a room.
2. Explain the value of completing one-fourth-inch scale drawings of rooms to be furnished.

Skill Objective

1. Using a one-fourth-inch scale, accurately reproduce a floor plan of a given room.

ASSIGNMENTS

Before Viewing the Program

□ Read pages 49–64 in the text, noting particularly those terms listed in the glossary in this lesson.
□ Read the comprehension and skill objectives for this lesson in the study guide.
□ Carefully study the overview, highlighting the important points and new concepts.
□ Look over the study activities and study questions for this lesson.

View the Program "Mapping It Out"

While viewing the program, note specifically:

□ the special equipment which is helpful in preparing scale-drawn floor plans.
□ the demonstration of how to use this equipment to center and draw a floor plan.
□ architectural and electrical symbols used in a detailed floor plan.
□ the advantage of using wall elevations as well as floor plans.
□ architects Sushi Kishiyama and Peter Ostrander describing the process of developing complete plans for clients.

After Viewing the Program

□ Review the glossary terms and learning objectives.

□ Complete the study activities.
□ Test your understanding of this lesson by answering the study questions at the end of the lesson. Check your answers with the key.

GLOSSARY

(Page numbers refer to your text.)

architectural scale: a three-sided ruler used to measure and draw accurate floor plans.

architectural symbols, page 55

blueprints, page 55

closed plan, page 61

electrical symbols: markings used on architectural drawings to indicate the placement of electrical lights, outlets, and switches. See Figure 6.1.

elevation drawings: scale drawings showing the arrangement of furnishings against each wall in a room.

one-fourth-inch scale: the accepted proportion used to measure and draw accurate floor plans.

open plan, page 61

standard milled items, page 52

templates: small patterns of furniture used as guides in planning room arrangements.

STUDY ACTIVITIES

Required Activities

1. Accurately reproduce to one-fourth-inch scale a floor plan for one room you will be furnishing. Include all essential architectural and electrical symbols.
2. Using the floor plan drawn in the first activity, complete the one-fourth-inch scale elevation drawing of one wall that has at least one architectural detail, such as a fireplace, door, window, or built-in unit.

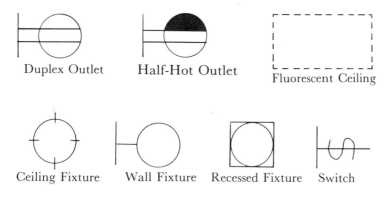

Duplex Outlet   Half-Hot Outlet   Fluorescent Ceiling

Ceiling Fixture   Wall Fixture   Recessed Fixture   Switch

FIGURE 6.1. Electrical Symbols

Extra-Credit Activities

1. Write a one-to-two page paper explaining two reasons for completing a scale floor-plan drawing of a room you plan to furnish.
2. Using the following measurements, draw lines indicating their conversion to one-fourth-inch scale: 6′2″, 2′6″, 15′, and 7′10″.

STUDY QUESTIONS

(Select the one best answer.)

Comprehension Objective 1: Identify and accurately describe all architectural and electrical symbols used to draw a scale floor plan for a room.

1. What does the following symbol indicate on an architectural drawing?

   a. wall fixture
   b. ceiling fixture
   c. wall switch
   d. duplex outlet

Match the name of the architectural and electrical symbols on the right to the symbols on the left by writing the corresponding number in the blanks provided.

   a. fluorescent ceiling
   b. standard window
   c. ceiling fixture
   d. french doors
   e. recessed fixture
   f. standard lavatory

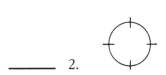

_____ 2.

_____ 3.

_____ 4.

_____ 5.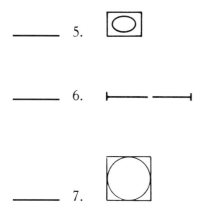

_____ 6. ⊢—— ——⊣

_____ 7.

Comprehension Objective 2:   Explain the value of completing one-fourth-inch scale drawings of rooms to be furnished.

8. The first step in developing a successfully planned room is to
   a. visualize a picture of the end result.
   b. have everything color coordinated.
   c. make a scale drawing of the floor plan of the room.
   d. establish the furniture arrangement.

9. Having a scale-drawn interior design plan will help you to
   a. develop a comfortable furniture arrangement.
   b. evaluate the flow of traffic through the room.
   c. avoid impulse buying.
   d. accomplished all of the above.
   e. accomplish the goals described in a and b.

ANSWER KEY

(Page numbers refer to your text.)

1. d (study guide)
2. c (study guide)
3. b (page 55)
4. a (study guide)
5. f (page 55)
6. d (page 55)
7. e (study guide)
8. c (study guide, television program)
9. d (study guide, television program)

ENLIGHTEN YOUR HOME

OVERVIEW

Lighting is the magic tool that can take a pleasantly designed interior plan and turn it into an outstanding design, one that delights the eye and beckons all to enter and enjoy the surroundings. No matter how well a room is decorated, much of its design impact is lost if the lighting throughout is insufficient or unplanned. Careful selection and control of artificial illumination and use of natural daylight will affect the beauty, safety, and function of an interior environment. This lesson will help you to understand why lighting never should be left as an "afterthought" in designing.

Development of a lighting plan begins with understanding the lighting needs which are dictated by the activities that will occur in the room. To meet those needs, a designer will plan to provide three different types of lighting. **Ambient lighting**—the low level that illuminates an entire room—creates the overall lighting mood and meets usual lighting needs. This type of lighting should be evenly distributed. **Task lighting**—additional illumination for specific activities such as reading or sewing—supplements the general lighting plan. Task lighting is best controlled through dimmers or three-way switches. **Accent lighting**, used to highlight art objects and paintings or to emphasize wall areas, creates dramatic effects and focuses attention on interesting areas or objects.

Lighting should be balanced in a room the same way that you would balance the visual weight of your furniture. In developing a lighting plan, remember that different rooms require different types and degrees of lighting. Illuminating engineers have found that the proper light for a given task can relax and refresh, while poor or incorrectly planned lighting can cause fatigue and irritation.

Several other specific factors need to be considered in developing a lighting plan: (1) the room plan and location of electrical outlets, (2) the activity lighting requirements, (3) the role natural light plays in the room, and (4) the theme or mood of the interior plan. A scale-drawn floor plan will act as the starting point for your lighting plan. Using your activity list as a guideline, develop your lighting plan by categorizing the task or accent lighting needed in each area of the room.

Whether you are planning a new house or making changes in an existing one, take a daytime and a nighttime inventory of the room's lighting needs. The mood you wish to create within the room should also be an important consideration in your plan. A mood that is quiet, serene, and restful is easily created with low-intensity lighting while a lively, cheerful mood is created with a higher lighting level.

After thinking through your lighting needs, you are ready to select appropriate light fixtures. **Incandescent lighting** is most commonly used in residences; however, incandescent bulbs cast a yellowish tint and may weaken colors in the blue-violet range. Incandescent bulbs are either standard or long-life, and come in wattages from ten to three hundred. It should be noted that wattage is the amount of electricity going into the light bulb; it is not a measure of the light emitted. Long-life bulbs have filaments that are heavier and thus will last approximately three times longer than standard bulbs. However, long-life bulbs give less light, three hundred fewer lumens than standard bulbs of the same wattage.

Another lighting option is energy-saving bulbs that consume eight percent less electricity yet provide the same amount of light as conventional wattage bulbs. They have a higher initial cost, but they are more economical because they use less electricity.

Fluorescent lighting is available in tube form and in variations of wattage and color. Fluorescent light is less flexible than incandescent because tubes of different wattages are not interchangeable within the same fixture (the longer the tube, the higher the wattage). However, fluorescent lights produce three to four times the light produced by incandescents of the same wattage, last seven to ten times longer, and use less energy. Most fluorescents in use today have a bluish cast that reduces the vitality of warm colors and is unflattering to complexions. However, some fluorescent lights have been "color improved" so that colors look more natural. These fluorescent lights may be used and blended with incandescent light.

A trend in lighting is toward the **structural** or built-in: a fixture or unit built directly into a ceiling, wall, window frame, or furniture. The principal advantage of structural lighting is that it offers superior light distribution. It also can be custom built to your requirements and takes up little or no space. Moreover, built-in lighting has no cords and actually enhances the architectural character of your home.

If you move frequently or rent, however, you may want to purchase **portable lighting** fixtures that you can unplug and move to another room or house. While a wide variety of portable fixtures are on the market, the most common are table or desk lamps, swag lamps, floor lamps, and some wall lamps. When choosing portable lighting for a particular situation, you should be aware of its value not only as task and accent lighting but also as a vital decorative accessory. Therefore, consider the theme of the area in which this lighting source will be used.

All lamps must have shades to diffuse light and prevent glare. Lamp shades vary widely in size, color, and translucency, but your choice should suit the scale of your lamp base and be in keeping with the general decorating scheme. The degree of translucency in the shades will be determined by the purpose of the lighting. Lamp shades of a light color provide the best lighting, but more dramatic effects can be achieved if one shade in a room is opaque.

If you do decide to include some structural lighting in a rented dwelling, it is advisable to obtain the owner's written permission before proceeding. However, you can simulate the effect of built-in lighting with portable canister lights or with spotlights that sit on the floor. Track lighting can be attached to walls or the ceiling and taken with you when you leave.

By learning to work with the elements of lighting you can create a plan that is both artistic and functional. Experiment with warm- and cool-colored bulbs. Change lighting angles from front to side and notice the changes in shadows. Observe how lighting contrast can be used to create drama or focus attention through highlights and shadows. Check the composition of your lighting plan: Do the pools of light lead people from one area to another in a stepping-stone fashion that projects warmth and hospitality?

The primary consideration in planning, selecting, and using lighting is the effectiveness of the light produced, not the appearance of the light fixture. When light is used creatively it can add function, dimension, and drama to any design plan.

LEARNING OBJECTIVES

After reading the assignment, viewing the program, and completing the assigned activities, you will be able to accomplish the following objectives:

Comprehension Objectives

1. Explain how well-planned lighting relates to the beauty, safety, and function of a room.
2. Identify at least four factors to consider when determining the type and amount of light needed in a room.
3. Define and explain two advantages and two disadvantages of both incandescent and fluorescent residential lighting.

Skill Objectives

1. Select a furnished room and activity list and identify the needs for both general and specific task lighting.
2. Design a lighting plan for a rental unit that uses only portable fixtures.

ASSIGNMENTS

Before Viewing the Program

- ☐ Read pages 84–98 in the text, noting particularly those terms listed in the glossary in this lesson.
- ☐ Read the comprehension and skill objectives for this lesson in the study guide.
- ☐ Carefully study the overview, highlighting the important points and new concepts.
- ☐ Look over the study activities and study questions for this lesson.

View the Program "Enlighten Your Home"

While viewing the program, note specifically:

- ☐ guest host Tom Martin explaining how to evaluate the effect of a lighting fixture, not just its style.
- ☐ examples of the three general categories of light and the function of each type.
- ☐ how color, angle, contrast, and composition affect lighting.
- ☐ the various instruments of lighting and type of light they produce.
- ☐ the advantages and disadvantages of incandescent and fluorescent lighting.
- ☐ the steps to take in developing a successful lighting plan.
- ☐ examples of the role natural light plays in lighting effects.
- ☐ the importance of the "mood" of lighting.

After Viewing the Program

- ☐ Review the glossary terms and learning objectives.
- ☐ Complete the study activities.
- ☐ Test your understanding of this lesson by answering the study questions at the end of the lesson. Check your answers with the key.

GLOSSARY

(Page numbers refer to your text.)

accent lighting, page 84

ambient lighting, page 84

base lighting, page 89

bracket lighting, page 87

canopy lighting, page 87

combustion lighting, page 92

cornice lighting, page 87

cove lighting, page 87

diffused light, page 84

direct lighting, page 93

downlights, page 89

fluorescent, page 93

incandescent, page 92

indirect lighting, page 93

lamp, page 84

lumens: a unit of measurement that indicates how much light radiates from a bulb.

luminaire, page 84

luminous ceiling, page 89

portable lighting, page 89

soffit lighting, page 89

structural lighting, page 87

task lighting, 84

valence lighting, page 87

STUDY ACTIVITIES

Required Activities

1. Develop a plan that uses both architectural and portable lighting sources to satisfy the needs of a combination kitchen/family room.

2. Using the one-bedroom unit floor plan on page 63 of your text, create a portable lighting plan for this unit as a rental dwelling. Use numbered symbols to show the lighting position on the floor plan and include a list, also numbered, to describe the activities to be performed in these numbered areas and the lighting fixtures to be purchased.

3. Choose one of the following activities to complete. Write a two-page paper describing your conclusions.
   □ Explain how well-planned lighting pertains to a room's function, beauty, and safety.
   □ Visit a major department store and notice the use of fluorescent and incandescent lights. Where is one type used almost exclusively? Why?

▫ Examine the types of lighting fixtures throughout your own home. Do they function as well as you planned? How could you improve the situation?

Extra-Credit Activities

1. List several advantages and disadvantages of incandescent and fluorescent lighting.
2. Name five methods of artificial lighting and describe a specific use for each type.
3. Compare the advantages and disadvantages of architectural and portable lighting.

STUDY QUESTIONS

(Select the one best answer.)

Comprehension Objective 1:   Explain how well-planned lighting relates to the beauty, safety, and function of a room.

1. A good lighting plan will
   a. improve household safety.
   b. bring art objects, plants, or paintings into focus.
   c. enhance colors and textures.
   d. provide an atmosphere of formality or intimacy as desired.
   e. do all of the above.

Match the types of lighting on the right that are best suited for the activities or purposes on the left by writing the corresponding letters in the blanks provided.

_____ 2. grooming	a. ambient	
_____ 3. ironing	b. task	
_____ 4. highlighting specific items	c. accent	
_____ 5. dining		
_____ 6. writing		
_____ 7. television viewing		
_____ 8. creating dramatic effects		
_____ 9. entertaining		
_____ 10. cooking		

11. The first step in developing a good lighting plan is to
    a. budget the necessary funds.
    b. purchase the needed fixtures.
    c. evaluate your lighting needs.
    d. assess the natural lighting.

Comprehension Objective 2:   Identify at least four factors to consider when determining the type and amount of light needed in a room.

12. Which of the following factors is *not* an essential consideration in developing a functional, well-planned lighting design?
    a. mood or atmosphere
    b. style of lighting fixtures
    c. daytime and nighttime lighting needs
    d. the role of natural lighting
    e. location of electrical outlets and switches

13. The type of lighting which can be most precisely controlled to provide the desired intensity and emphasis is
    a. incandescent lighting.
    b. task lighting.
    c. accent lighting.
    d. fluorescent lighting.

14. The best source of lighting for a bathroom sink area would be
    a. soffit lighting.
    b. canopy lighting.
    c. a luminous ceiling.
    d. any of the above.
    e. either soffit or canopy lighting.

15. A chandelier lighting fixture is an example of
    a. portable lighting.
    b. architectural lighting.
    c. a downlight.
    d. soffit lighting.

Comprehension Objective 3:   Define and explain two advantages and two disadvantages of both incandescent and fluorescent residential lighting.

16. The three sources of artificial light are
    a. general, task, and accent.
    b. combustion, incandescence, and luminescence.
    c. direct, indirect, and diffused.
    d. ambient, direct, and task.

17. Incandescent lighting is more _____ than fluorescent lighting.
    a. energy efficient
    b. controllable
    c. flattering
    d. controllable and flattering
    e. energy efficient, controllable, and flattering

18. What are two advantages of fluorescent light?
    a. It is quiet and inexpensive.
    b. It uses less energy and emits less heat.
    c. It is very flexible and portable.
    d. It is flattering and energy efficient.

ANSWER KEY

(Page numbers refer to your text.)

1. e (page 84)
2. b (pages 84, 86, and 97)
3. b (pages 84, 86, and 97)
4. c (pages 84, 86, and 97)
5. a (pages 84, 86, and 97)
6. b (pages 84, 86, and 97)
7. a (pages 84, 86, and 97)
8. c (pages 84, 86, and 97)
9. a (pages 84, 86, and 97)
10. b (pages 84, 86, and 97)
11. c (study guide, television program)
12. b (television program)
13. c (page 86)
14. d (page 89)
15. a (page 89)
16. b (page 92)
17. d (study guide, television program)
18. b (page 93)

FOCUS ON COLOR

OVERVIEW

Color is usually considered the most dynamic and important element in interior design. Although not everyone perceives color in the same way, all people are affected by their own physical and psychological interpretations of color. To use color effectively, it is essential to develop a thorough understanding of color dimensions—**hue**, **value**, and **intensity**—so that you can create color plans that elicit the visual and psychological responses desired by each individual within your home.

An introductory interior design course cannot present everything there is to know about color, but studying the vocabulary, function, effects, and the general guidelines for the use of color will provide a good basis for expanding your knowledge and understanding of color. To develop confidence in working within these guidelines, begin to look at color in new ways. Notice how it affects people in fashion, nature, business, travel, and recreation. Observe the effects of color in rough and smooth textures, of color in natural and artificial light, and advancing and receding colors. Study how colors relate to one another, remembering that it is difficult to evaluate colors without comparing them to other colors.

Your text and the television program compare the two color systems most commonly used in interior design: the **Brewster System**, which is based on pigments, and the **Munsell System**, which is based on light. While the Brewster System (represented by the standard color wheel) is helpful in gaining an understanding of the basic hues and their relationships, the Munsell System (illustrated by the triangular color globe) is more beneficial when analyzing variations in the value and intensity (chroma) of the specific hues.

The program "Focus on Color" explains how variations in color dimensions can produce illusory changes in a room setting and, in turn, how these visual effects can influence a person in that room. Walls treated with a light value of a **cool color** will tend to visually enlarge a room, which makes this type of treatment ideal for a person who requires a feeling of open space. This treatment, however, would not be a wise choice for one who prefers a "closed-in," more protected, environment.

While it is quite possible to plan a well-designed room in opposition to the color application guidelines, beginners generally find it easier to create a rewarding color plan by adhering to the specific hue, value, and intensity distribution guidelines presented in your text and the television program. Once you have developed confidence in working within these guidelines, experiment by varying—or even ignoring—the suggestions. For example, try using the most intense color on a large upholstered piece of furniture. Sometimes breaking a rule can be very effective aesthetically. However, to avoid expensive mistakes, experiment in the planning stage, mentally visualizing the room and evaluating the effects prior to making any purchases. Always use accurate color samples, the larger the better. To fully understand the application of your new color knowledge you must practice and experiment with color and evaluate the results.

LEARNING OBJECTIVES

After reading the assignment, viewing the program, and completing the assigned activities, you will be able to accomplish the following objectives:

Comprehension Objectives

1. Identify the three basic divisions of hues on a standard twelve-color wheel.
2. Define the following color dimensions: hue, value, and intensity.
3. Compare and contrast the Munsell and Brewster Color Systems.
4. Discuss the importance of considering lighting, texture, distance, and area when planning color for interiors.
5. Define the "Law of Chromatic Distribution" and explain how this law should be applied when planning color placement throughout a room.

Skill Objectives

1. Given five examples of room color plans, identify monochromatic, accented neutral, analogous, complementary, and triad color schemes.
2. Given a basic item such as a rug, wallpaper, or upholstery fabric, explain how you would proceed to develop a color planning board.
3. Using tempera paints, create a standard color wheel starting with the three primary colors and ending with twelve.
4. Using tempera paints, illustrate how tones, tints, and shades vary in value distribution and neutralization.

ASSIGNMENTS

Before Viewing the Program

□ Read pages 101–131 in the text, noting particularly those items listed in the glossary in this lesson.
□ Read the comprehension and skill objectives for this lesson in the study guide.
□ Carefully study the overview, highlighting the important points and new concepts.
□ Look over the study activities and study questions for this lesson.

View the Program "Focus on Color"

While viewing the program, note specifically:

□ the basic divisions of a standard color wheel and the effect of mixing a given color with black, white, gray, or a complementary color.

□ the five color harmonies found in nature and how they may be used in an interior setting.

□ how color schemes are created through the use of color application guidelines suggested in this lesson.

□ how to use dominant and subordinate colors in two- or three-color combinations.

□ the effects of value, intensity, and chromatic distribution that need to be considered when developing a color plan.

□ the application and use of warm and cool colors, how texture affects color, ways lighting can be used to create optical illusions, and how even so-called "neutral" colors have underlying tones of warm or cool colors.

□ how to use color samples or a "color planning board."

After Viewing the Program

□ Review the glossary terms and learning objectives.

□ Complete the study activities.

□ Test your understanding of this lesson by answering the study questions at the end of the lesson. Check your answers with the key.

GLOSSARY

(Page numbers refer to your text.)

Brewster System, page 104

chromatic distribution, page 124

color schemes, page 114

    achromatic

    analogous

    complementary

    monochromatic

cool colors, page 103

hue, page 108

intensity, page 108

Munsell System, page 104

primary, page 106

secondary, page 106

shade, page 108

Shibui, page 128

tertiary, page 106

tint, page 108

tone, page 108

value distribution, page 124

warm colors, page 103

STUDY ACTIVITIES

Required Activities

1. Complete Color Cards One, Two, Three, Four, Five, Six, and Seven in your student packet. Follow the directions listed on pages 130–131 in your text.
2. Complete two of the following activities and write a one-to-two-page paper with your answers or comments.
    □ Compare Figures 5.16 and 5.17 in your text. Describe how the colors and lighting affect the mood of the room. Which treatment do you prefer? Why?
    □ Describe two ways one color can be used to help increase the apparent intensity of another color.
    □ Give an example of how color can be used to solve each of the following room problems:
    >   The ceiling is too high.
    >   The room is too small.
    >   The room has a structural component in an undesirable color.
    >   The room is very long and narrow.
    □ Explain the importance of evaluating color samples in the location in which they will be used.
    □ Study the color schemes used in the text illustrations listed below. Identify each of the following by matching the name to the illustration.

analogous	Figure 5.1, page 100
accented neutral	Figure 6.1, page 134
complementary	Figure 10.1, page 266
monochromatic	Figure 10.8, page 285
triad	Figure 11.5, page 295

Extra-Credit Activities

1. Visit a model home or design showhouse, noting how color is used to create a mood, for transition, as emphasis, or to minimize a flaw. Go through each room twice. Did your reaction change the second time? What did you notice the second time that was overlooked the first? How did the color schemes relate to your personal taste? Write a two-page paper describing the exhibit and your reactions.
2. Complete the exercise described above, using the text illustrations listed in the last assignment of required activity 2.

STUDY QUESTIONS

(Select the one best answer.)

Comprehension Objective 1:   Identify the three basic divisions of hues on a standard twelve-color wheel.

   Match the colors on the right with the appropriate division on a standard color wheel on the left by writing the corresponding letters in the blanks provided.

———— 1. primary   a. orange, green, violet

———— 2. secondary   b. red, blue, yellow

———— 3. tertiary   c. orange, blue

———— 4. analogous   d. yellow, yellow-green, green

———— 5. complementary   e. red-violet, blue-violet

6. A standard twelve-color wheel is divided into three basic divisions; they are:
   a. primary, secondary, complementary colors.
   b. primary, secondary, tertiary colors.
   c. tints, tones, and shades.
   d. hue, value, intensity.

7. Equal amounts of primary and secondary colors combine to form
   a. gray.
   b. tertiary colors.
   c. neutral colors.
   d. shaded colors.

Comprehension Objective 2:   Define the following color dimensions: hue, value, and intensity.

8. The term "hue" refers to
   a. full intensity.
   b. a dark value.
   c. a color name.
   d. a color wheel.

9. Value in relation to color refers to
   a. the degree of luminosity.
   b. the lightness or darkness of a color.
   c. gradation of color ranging from white to black.
   d. all of the above.

10. Tints and shades of a hue are synonymous with
    a. color intensity.
    b. color value.
    c. the Prang System.
    d. chroma.

11. The brightness or dullness and strength or weakness of a color describes the property known as
    a. hue.
    b. value.
    c. shade.
    d. chroma or intensity.

Comprehension Objective 3:   Compare and contrast the Munsell and Brewster Color Systems.

12. The Munsell Color System is based on the description and analysis of color according to three attributes:
    a. tone, shade, tint.
    b. black, white, gray.
    c. hue, value, intensity.
    d. monochromatic, achromatic, analogous.

13. Three primary pigment colors can be combined to create three secondary and six tertiary colors, producing a twelve-color system known as
    a. the Brewster System.
    b. the Prang System.
    c. the standard color wheel.
    d. all of the above.

Comprehension Objective 4: Discuss the importance of considering lighting, texture, distance, and area when planning color for interiors.

14. The importance of lighting and its effect on color have been reduced because modern textile dye methods have produced colors that are exactly the same under natural and artificial light sources.
    a. true
    b. false

15. Which colors have visually advancing qualities that may be used in a large room to make it appear more cozy?
    a. primary
    b. secondary
    c. warm
    d. cool

16. Color applied to a rough, uneven textured surface will appear _____ that applied to smooth surfaces.
    a. lighter in color than
    b. darker in color than
    c. more intense than
    d. about the same as

Comprehension Objective 5: Define the "Law of Chromatic Distribution" and explain how this law should be applied when planning color placement throughout a room.

17. The "Law of Chromatic Distribution" suggests the use of color following which of these guidelines?
    a. dark backgrounds, light furniture, and subtle accents
    b. neutral backgrounds, furniture with more intensity, and accents in strongest intensity
    c. light backgrounds, dark furniture, and dark floors
    d. shaded backgrounds, furniture in tints, and accents in metallic tones

18. As areas decrease in size, the chromatic intensity of colors may be increased according to which of these theories?
    a. Brewster Color System
    b. Munsell Color System
    c. Law of Chromatic Distribution
    d. Shibui color concept

ANSWER KEY

(Page numbers refer to your text.)

1. b (pages 105–106, television program)
2. a (pages 105–106, television program)
3. e (page 106, television program)
4. d (page 114, television program)
5. c (pages 114–115, television program)
6. b (pages 104–105, television program)
7. b (page 105, television program)
8. c (page 108, television program)
9. d (page 108, television program)

10. b (page 108, television program)
11. d (page 111, television program)
12. c (pages 106–114)
13. d (pages 104–106)
14. b (pages 119–121)
15. c (television program)
16. b (page 121, television program)
17. b (pages 124–127)
18. c (pages 124–127)

COLOR WITH CONFIDENCE

OVERVIEW

Creating an esthetically pleasing **color plan** for an entire home or even for just one room is a challenging task. Understanding the theory and psychology of color is helpful when the decision-making stage of color selection occurs, but before these decisions are made several important factors should be considered. The program for this lesson, "Color with Confidence," introduces Gwen, an interior designer who is working with the Anderson family to develop a color plan for their new home.

Although there is no rigid list of steps to follow when developing a color plan, most professional designers follow basic general procedures. They begin by assessing a family's needs and preferences, then they gather color samples of paint, fabric, wall and floor coverings, evaluate the samples in the home setting, and formulate a color plan. Using the selected samples, designers work with clients to assess the plan and revise it when necessary. Finally, the purchasing stage begins. The methodical care with which the preliminary steps have been accomplished should help prevent mistakes and disappointments during this stage. Gwen follows these basic procedures, beginning with the assessment, or "detective," stage through the final purchases for her clients.

In planning your own family's color plan, these same steps should prove to be helpful. During the detective stage, gather facts about the people who will occupy your home, their life styles, color preferences, desired mood or theme, personal needs, and budget limitations. For example, if you have a mobile life style, you might need to select more neutral or versatile colors for major furniture pieces than if you were developing a plan for a permanent residence. Also, it is a good idea to think through several variations of the basic **color scheme** using this same furniture.

During the initial planning stage, it is essential to assess the housing site in order to understand interior architectural considerations as well as variations in natural lighting. Once you have made this assessment, you can choose one of many methods to create a living color scheme. Your text suggests several methods on page 115.

Remember that a beautiful color scheme is the result of incorporating several important considerations into one plan. For example, a color scheme frequently loses its charm when the family discovers that particular color choices require excessive maintenance. Similarly, a color plan that looks perfect in natural lighting may appear dull or look entirely different under artificial lights.

Solid colors sometimes provide more opportunities for variations in a color plan than do patterned materials. This factor is important not only to those who have mobile life styles, but also to those families preferring to make more frequent changes in their decor. A patterned wall covering, a few new accessories, and a different paint color are a few of the inexpensive yet effective ways to revitalize a room that has relatively simple, understated furniture pieces.

You may be tempted to base your schemes on current color trends or **fads**. When the market is saturated with products in specific colors, consumers tend to select those colors not so much because they express personal preferences, but because they are readily available and are marketed to capture the consumer's attention. Keep in mind that, as with all fashions, the popularity of specific colors changes fairly rapidly, and these colors may lose their personal appeal within a very few years. In addition, once a color is no longer "in," it is difficult to find replacements for worn items or new pieces that coordinate with the original color scheme.

To make the most accurate evaluation of your plans before purchasing, you should request loan samples for such items as wall coverings, carpeting, or fabrics. Some retailers allow you to check out a sample directly; others will order a small loan sample for your use. These samples allow you to evaluate colors in the setting in which they will be used and to determine how all the selections for one room relate to each other. The samples should be large enough to show all the dominant colors in each major area (wall coverings, flooring, predominant wood tones, and others) and should be grouped together to represent each room. Ideally, the sample sizes should be proportionate to the extent in which they are used in the room.

Throughout the planning stage, check your plan for continuity of color, smooth **transition**, and variety in textures and pattern. Keep revising and replacing samples until your plan reflects your family's taste and life style.

After you have developed a complete color plan, you will be ready for the decision-making stage. You may want to divide your purchasing into several budget stages. However, in the months ahead, when you will be ready to buy, some of your original choices of colors, fabrics, or carpeting could be discontinued. Although it is usually possible to find suitable substitutions for your original selections, if there are particular ones you feel you must have, purchase these first.

LEARNING OBJECTIVES

After reading the assignment, viewing the program, and completing the assigned activities, you will be able to accomplish the following objectives:

Comprehension Objectives

1. Identify and define the four basic types of color schemes.
2. Describe the effect of adjacent colors on each other.
3. Identify and apply an effective, step-by-step approach to planning an interior color scheme.

Skill Objectives

1. Applying one of the suggested approaches for developing a color scheme, suggest a complete color plan for a room.
2. Select a room and specify the following functions for the room: desired theme or mood, needed visible changes, and psychological and personal color preferences.
3. Given a picture of a room, develop a transitional color plan that conforms with the principles of design for an adjacent room.

ASSIGNMENTS

Before Viewing the Program

□ Review pages 114–131 from "Color Schemes" through the end of the chapter in the text, noting particularly those terms listed in the glossary in this lesson.
□ Read the comprehension and skill objectives for this lesson in the study guide.
□ Carefully study the overview, highlighting the important points and new concepts.
□ Look over the study activities and study questions for this lesson.

View the Program "Color with Confidence"

While viewing the program, note specifically:

□ the facts that need to be gathered to establish a basis for a color plan.
□ the effects of natural and artificial lighting on color.
□ how to have continuity and transition in a plan so that it does not become monotonous.
□ how Gwen, the interior designer, develops a color scheme for her clients, the Anderson family.
□ television instructor Winnie Yablonski reviewing five steps in developing a color plan.

After Viewing the Program

□ Review the glossary terms and learning objectives.
□ Complete the study activities.
□ Test your understanding of this lesson by answering the study questions at the end of the lesson. Check your answers with the key.

GLOSSARY

(Page numbers refer to your text.)

color-plan development steps: a suggested procedure for successfully creating a color plan, starting with assessing family preferences, gathering and evaluating sample colors, formulating a color plan, evaluating the plan, revising the plan, and implementing the final choices.

color fads: currently popular colors and color schemes in furnishings and fashions.

color transition: page 122

complete color plan: samples showing the actual colors and patterns used in an interior design plan including paint, wallpaper, fabric, wood, tile, brick, and floor coverings.

contrasting color scheme, page 114

related color scheme, page 114

swatch file: color samples of wall, floor, and furniture coverings that are being considered for inclusion in a color plan.

Review the following terms from Lesson Eight:

color schemes, page 114
- □ **achromatic**
- □ **analogous**
- □ **complementary**
- □ **monochromatic**

Shibui, page 128

STUDY ACTIVITIES

Required Activities

1. Complete Plates 8, 9, and 10 in the student packet, following the directions given on page 131 of your test.
2. Select *one* illustration from Figures 6.1, 6.8, and 6.9 and discuss the following points in relation to use of color within that room:
   - □ theme or mood.
   - □ visual effects produced by specific values and intensities.
   - □ hue, value, and intensity distribution.
   - □ possible psychological reactions of those living in the room.
3. Choose one of the following assignments to complete:
   - □ Write a brief definition of transitional color planning. Then, using Figure 5.15, write a one-to-two page analysis of how color transition was achieved in the two rooms illustrated.
   - □ Using pictures of an upholstered sofa and one chair, each in different colors, develop a color plan that successfully incorporates these two pieces into one room.

Extra-Credit Activity

1. View the furnishing displays in several department or furniture stores and write a short paper discussing the current color trends or "fads." Basing your conclusions on your observations and opinions, explain what changes will be seen in popular use within the next three years.

STUDY QUESTIONS

(Select the one best answer.)

Comprehension Objective 1:   Identify and define the four basic types of color schemes.

1. Which of the following is (are) (a) distinguishing characteristic(s) of a monochromatic color scheme?
   a. all colors of the same intensity
   b. monotony
   c. unity
   d. all of the above characteristics
   e. the characteristics described in a and c

2. Which of the following groups of colors represents an achromatic color scheme?
    a. gray, black, and white
    b. beige, brown, and black
    c. white, beige, and brown
    d. beige and brown, with accents of soft pastel colors

3. A color scheme drawn from a group of adjacent colors on a standard wheel is called
    a. monochromatic.
    b. analogous.
    c. achromatic.
    d. complementary.

4. Which of the following would be an example of a complementary color scheme?
    a. a bedroom with all furnishings in shades or rose and mauve
    b. a kitchen in orange, yellow, and green
    c. a living room with all furnishings in the same hue, with variety produced by varying color intensities and textures
    d. a child's bedroom with red and blue predominating

5. According to your text, which color scheme offers the most variety?
    a. achromatic
    b. analogous
    c. complementary
    d. monochromatic

Comprehension Objective 2:   Describe the effect of adjacent colors on each other.

6. When the primary colors red and blue are placed next to each other they will appear to be tinted with
    a. purple.
    b. yellow.
    c. green.
    d. red-orange and aqua-blue.

7. When using two strong contrasting or complementary colors together, it is important that they be
    a. of different value.
    b. of the same value.
    c. either adjacent or directly opposite on the color wheel.
    d. used in different proportions.
    e. of the same value but used in different proportions.

Match adjacent colors on the left with the descriptions of their effects on the right by writing the corresponding letters in the blanks provided.

_____ 8. red and green of equal intensity	a. appears light
_____ 9. gray on a white background	b. appears dark
_____ 10. gray on a black background	c. fatigues the viewer
_____ 11. blue on a gray background	d. stands out
_____ 12. red on a gray background	e. blends into the background

13. A client insists on using an unattractive peach-colored chair in her spacious living room. You can minimize the visual impact of this piece by positioning it
    a. in front of a wall painted a similar shade of peach.
    b. in front of a window with striped draperies.
    c. on a wall covered with vivid wallpaper, with peach a predominant color.
    d. in front of a wall painted light blue.

Comprehension Objective 3:   Identify and apply an effective, step-by-step approach to planning an interior color scheme.

14. The inspiration for an interior color plan might come from
    a. a prized picture.
    b. a color scheme copied from a magazine, model home, or furniture store showroom.
    c. selecting a favorite color and bringing in other colors to blend.
    d. any or all of the above.

15. A primary consideration in planning a color scheme for a room is
    a. to match the draperies to the wall color.
    b. the quality and quantity of natural light available.
    c. the floor covering.
    d. any architectural feature of the home.

16. A formal, conservative atmosphere in a dining room could best be achieved by using
    a. dark-colored shag rugs.
    b. chocolate brown burlap-textured wall coverings.
    c. cream-colored wallpaper with a subtle off-white stripe.
    d. red flocked wallpaper with gold accents.

17. Shibui refers to
    a. A Chinese approach to beauty.
    b. camouflaging architectural flaws.
    c. using dominant colors in the largest areas.
    d. the tranquil, serene application of colors and textures found in nature.

18. A final color plan should be developed before gathering color samples.
    a. true
    b. false

ANSWER KEY

(Page numbers refer to your text.)

1. c (page 114)
2. a (page 114)
3. b (page 114)
4. d (pages 114–115)
5. c (pages 114–115)
6. b (page 116)
7. a (page 116)
8. c (page 117)
9. b (page 117)

10. a (page 117)
11. e (page 117)
12. d (page 117)
13. a (page 117)
14. d (page 115)
15. b (page 118)
16. c (television program)
17. d (page 128)
18. b (television program)

SPACE PLANNING

OVERVIEW

Arranging the furnishings in a room may seem like a simple task, but the careful selection and placement of these furnishings can determine whether the final result is marvelous, mediocre, or mistaken. Careful design of the available space within a room begins, as with other aspects of design, with an accurate assessment of family needs and the incorporation of those needs into a comprehensive plan. Designing a **space plan** involves dividing and allocating space to provide for the movement and flow of traffic, creating activity areas, and developing a well-thought-out furniture arrangement.

Before determining an arrangement plan, however, you will need to study the interior space of the room or rooms and make a scale floor-plan drawing. Use the $1/4'' = 1''$ architectural scale to chart dimensions, accesses, openings, electrical outlets, and other fixed architectural features, and include these features in your plan as well.

After you have drawn your floor plan, divide the space into general **activity areas** and locate **traffic patterns**. Traffic lanes are the areas that need to be left open and unencumbered by furniture. Usually, the traffic patterns developed in each room subdivide the space into distinct and obvious zones.

When this logical subdivision occurs, the task of **activity planning** is simplified considerably. The purpose of activity planning is to chart the intended use of space and furniture requirements within a room. Each activity area demands individualized study in which the needs of those persons using the space influence the choice of furniture, color, and materials. In this stage of planning, it is necessary to allow enough room for each activity. The **minimum clearances** given on page 286 in your text will be beneficial in planning activity spaces. At times an area may be large enough to allow for the separation of all activities; in other spaces, activities must overlap and rooms must meet a variety of purposes.

A successful furniture arrangement allows people to interact in a comfortable manner. To support this functional objective, the furniture-arrangement plan should provide needed seating space, surface space, and visual interest.

Once you have carefully considered and logically planned these aspects, you can turn your attention to aesthetics. The most important factors at this point include the relationship of the scale of furnishings to the available space, the contrast of horizontal and vertical elements, and the harmonious composition of furniture groupings.

As you work with these spaces within your home, you will find that rooms with similar dimensions may give very different space impressions. These impressions are directly related to the main entrance of the room; it is from this point that the room will be viewed most often. How spacious or how small the space seems is related to how far or near the opposite wall is to the doorway. Also, surface colors used for the walls, ceiling, and floor covering, combined with the amount of natural and artificial lighting in the room, all work together to create an impression of spaciousness or confinement. These space impressions are an important consideration related to the development of furniture-arrangement plans and color schemes.

Effective space planning and functional furniture arrangement deserve early and careful study, particularly in regard to your family's life style. Keep in mind that there is no one way to arrange a space; it is best to decide what is important to you and your family. You can then determine which plan allows the most comfortable and visually effective use of the available space.

LEARNING OBJECTIVES

After reading the assignment, viewing the program, and completing the assigned activities, you will be able to accomplish the following objectives:

Comprehension Objectives

1. Define the general goal of space planning.
2. Cite at least five functional considerations for furniture arrangement and explain how to evaluate each during the planning stage.
3. Identify and discuss the primary steps required to correctly complete a furniture arrangement plan.
4. Explain the relationship that room shape has to developing a satisfying furniture arrangement.

Skill Objectives

1. Given a floor plan, create a list of the functions and areas of activity, establish furniture needs, and develop a furniture-arrangement plan that satisfies the identified requirements.
2. Applying the principles of design, evaluate the floor and wall compositions of a specified furnished room. Suggest changes in the plan that would improve the total design.

ASSIGNMENTS

Before Viewing the Program

- Read pages 265–288 in your text, noting particularly those terms listed in the glossary in this lesson.
- Read the comprehension and skill objectives for this lesson in the study guide.

□ Carefully study the overview, highlighting the important points and new concepts.

□ Look over the study activities and study questions for this lesson.

View the Program "Space Planning"

While viewing the program, note specifically:

□ interior designer Jody Greenwald using templates, grid floor plans, and models to demonstrate the concepts of furniture arrangement.

□ the primary function of a successful furniture arrangement plan.

□ the basic needs which a well-planned arrangement of furniture should satisfy.

□ the sequence in which seating space, surface space, and visual impact are considered in developing a furniture arrangement.

□ how to create a satisfying conversation grouping.

□ the interrelationship between function and aesthetics in room planning.

□ the effect of lighting, accessories and storage pieces on the balance and proportion of a room.

□ the advantage of modular seating pieces for people with mobile life styles.

After Viewing the Program

□ Review the glossary terms and learning objectives.

□ Complete the study activities.

□ Test your understanding of this lesson by answering the study questions at the end of the lesson. Check your answers with the key.

GLOSSARY

(Page numbers refer to your text.)

activity areas: the localized spaces where specific functions are performed.

activity planning: charting the intended use of space and furniture within a specific room.

box-shaped grouping, pages 275 and 276

circular grouping, pages 275 and 276

L-shaped grouping, pages 275 and 276

minimum clearances, page 286

modular conversation grouping, pages 275 and 276

parallel grouping, pages 275 and 276

space planning, page 267

straight-line grouping, pages 275 and 276

traffic patterns: the path of movement followed as people move from one room to another or from one activity area to another within the same room.

U-shaped grouping, pages 275 and 276

STUDY ACTIVITIES

Required Activities

1. Using illustration 3 on page 287 in your text, list the functions and activities of the room. Rearrange the existing furnishings into a more pleasing plan.
2. Select a wall elevation in your home and create a picture arrangement for that wall. Draw a scale plan showing the shapes and sizes of the selections used in the picture grouping. Explain whether the arrangement is asymmetrical or bisymmetrical and why you chose that formation.

Extra-Credit Activities

1. Evaluate your own home and its functional qualities. Are there good traffic patterns? Does the furniture need rearranging? Are the activity areas well planned for maximum use?
2. Choose a room in your home that must be used for several different functions. Suggest other ways you might make this room a multipurpose room.

STUDY QUESTIONS

(Select the one best answer.)

Comprehension Objective 1:   Define the general goal of space planning.

1. The key word for any furniture arrangement plan in any room is
   a. economy.
   b. design.
   c. efficiency.
   d. unity.
2. Which of the following elements is *not* considered essential information in developing a space plan?
   a. division and allocation of space
   b. cost analysis and purchase plan
   c. activity planning
   d. furniture arrangement
   e. the direction and flow of traffic
3. The goal of good space planning is to
   a. reduce the final cost of your interior design plan.
   b. justify the cost of architectural changes.
   c. inspire a color scheme based on a specific theme.
   d. satisfy the need for easy mobility, comfort, and function.

Comprehension Objective 2:   Cite at least five functional considerations for furniture arrangement and explain how to evaluate each during the planning stage.

4. Good balance of furnishings in a room would include
   a. expensive and inexpensive furniture.
   b. bright and subdued colors.
   c. high and low pieces of furniture.
   d. angular and rounded pieces of furniture.
   e. the factors described in c and d.

5. Large pieces of furniture are best placed
   a. perpendicular to the wall.
   b. parallel to the wall.
   c. on a wall by themselves with no other furnishings.
   d. diagonally across a corner of a room.

6. An important consideration when designing a conversation grouping is to
   a. provide seating and surface space as well as visual interest.
   b. select restful, yet stimulating, colors
   c. separate individuals at least eight feet for good eye contact.
   d. provide both ambient and accent lighting.

Comprehension Objective 3:   Identify and discuss the primary steps required to correctly complete a furniture arrangement plan.

7. After assessing family needs, the next logical step in designing a furnishings plan is to
   a. list the furniture needed.
   b. establish traffic patterns.
   c. draw scale floor plans.
   d. allocate activity areas.

8. Which of the following elements is *not* essential to a floor plan?
   a. using a 1/4″ = 1′ scale
   b. the exact location of all doors, windows, radiators, heating vents
   c. built-in lights, switches, and outlets
   d. exact window and ceiling heights

9. The modular furniture grouping which provides flexible conversational seating in both large and small areas is
   a. straight-line.
   b. U-shaped.
   c. L-shaped.
   d. parallel.

Comprehension Objective 4:   Explain the relationship that room shape has to developing a satisfying furniture arrangement.

10. The room shape with the most pleasing proportion for decorating is
    a. rectangular.
    b. square.
    c. L-shaped.
    d. a room with a jog.

11. To provide a sense of balance and proportion in a long, narrow room,
    a. paint the long walls a darker color than the short walls.
    b. use high pieces of furniture to act as room dividers.
    c. place furniture at right angles to a long wall.
    d. do all of the above.
    e. use the techniques described in either b or c.

12. Which of the following furniture-arrangement techniques is (are) suitable for a square room?
    a. Build a bookshelf and cabinet arrangement the entire length of one wall.
    b. Use a rectangular area rug in one activity area.
    c. Use a sectional sofa to divide the room in half.
    d. Any of the above techniques is suitable.
    e. Only the techniques described in a and b are suitable.

ANSWER KEY

(Page numbers refer to your text.)

1. c (page 267)
2. b (study guide)
3. d (television program)
4. e (page 268)
5. b (page 268)
6. a (page 272, television program)
7. c (study guide, television program)
8. d (page 268)
9. c (page 275)
10. a (page 271)
11. e (pages 271–272)
12. e (page 271)

MAKE YOUR OWN ARRANGEMENT

OVERVIEW

Unique spaces that offer a real challenge to the designer include small apartments, compact dwellings such as **condominiums, townhouses,** or mobile homes, and even small alcoves and rooms in an average-sized room. These so-called "problem areas" usually must serve a variety of purposes within limited space—and therein lies the problem. But with careful furniture arrangement and the use of furniture that is flexible and adaptable, you can design a satisfactory environment in these small areas. This lesson, then, applies the techniques suggested in Lesson Ten, "Space Planning," to smaller areas.

In a smaller area it is particularly important to create and follow a furniture-arrangement plan. After you have established family needs, take one room at a time and analyze its anticipated uses. At this point it is wise to determine **alternative furniture arrangement** plans. Even though you feel you have developed the best furniture arrangement possible for a particular area, try to visualize the room used in a variety of situations. Often, simple rearrangement will allow a room to function better daytime *and* nighttime, in all seasons, and for a wide variety of activities, from family use to formal entertaining. Through wise planning and precise furnishing, you can expand limited space and increase its usefulness.

Keep in mind that planning the furnishing of small spaces requires practicality, flexibility, a working knowledge of the design elements, and especially accurate measurements. All furnishings, current and anticipated, fit the available space and must meet the needs of the individuals using that space. (Review pages 286–288 in your text for the minimum clearances necessary in a functional room.)

Furniture pieces should also be adaptable (preferably portable) to suit a number of needs throughout the overall design. If you buy temporary, or **"fill-in furniture,"** try to plan secondary uses for it. For example, an inexpensive living room sofa table later might become a desk in a child's room. Director's chairs are inexpensive and can be used temporarily in a living room, then later moved to the patio. One set of dining chairs could serve several functions. In addition to their primary function, they could be placed throughout the home as desk chairs, bedroom accessories, or additional seating in a conversation area. This **flexible planning** will not only save money but will also conserve valuable space. As a bonus, **adaptable furniture** pieces are assets to individuals who have mobile life styles. These furniture pieces can be moved easily, not only from room to room, but also from home to home.

Your text offers guidelines and suggestions for arranging furniture in specific rooms. (Refer to pages 272–278.) Adapt these guidelines to your own smaller rooms and, at the same time, blend function with beauty and comfort.

In many small dwellings, you may need to define **living zones** by "visually" dividing space. Furniture arrangement can easily accomplish this; for example, setting a sofa, several chairs, and a table on an area rug can unify an area even though it is not surrounded by four walls. Other items of furniture, such as bookcases, can be used to separate and define space.

Do not allow convention to dictate how you rearrange available space to suit your life style and needs. For instance, you may choose to disregard the traditional designations of living room and dining room and plan these areas for work, crafts, or even sleeping activities. However, you don't want to overlook the need for privacy in small dwellings as well as large.

Once you have developed a good, overall plan, you can establish priorities and plan items to add as your budget allows. Of course, the basics—furnishings that provide comfort and convenience—should be budgeted first and other items can be postponed. The logical progression in developing a budget with your plan in mind is from necessities to secondary furnishings to the final stage: the finishing touches of decorative or luxury items.

LEARNING OBJECTIVES

After reading the assignment, viewing the program, and completing the assigned activities, you will be able to accomplish the following objectives:

Comprehension Objectives

1. Describe the limitations and challenges of designing furniture arrangements for small-scaled dwellings.
2. Explain the importance of and techniques for developing adaptable furnishing plans for mobile life styles.
3. Cite five ideas that can be incorporated into a flexible, low-cost interior design plan.

Skill Objectives

1. Given a list of required furniture and proposed activities for a specific room, satisfy the needs of each activity by developing two alternate furniture arrangements.
2. Design a wall grouping using pictures, weavings, wall-hung accessories, or other artwork that would create a focal point in a small-scaled room.

ASSIGNMENTS

Before Viewing the Program

- Review pages 272–288 in the text, noting particularly those items listed in the glossary in this lesson.
- Read the comprehension and skill objectives for this lesson in the study guide.

□ Carefully study the overview, highlighting the important points and new concepts.

□ Look over the study activities and study questions for this lesson.

View the Program "Make Your Own Arrangement"

While viewing the program, note specifically:

□ how to develop a master plan for the purchase of major furnishings.

□ suggestions from the three guest designers, Joan Neville, Jackie Olmstead, and Hank Morgan, for selecting furniture styles and colors that provide flexibility in a mobile life style.

□ Ideas for decorating on a limited income, and when it is appropriate to buy quality furnishings.

After Viewing the Program

□ Review the glossary terms and learning objectives.

□ Complete the study activities.

□ Test your understanding of this lesson by answering the study questions at the end of the lesson. Check your answers with the key.

GLOSSARY

(Page numbers refer to your text.)

adaptable furnishings: furniture that can be used in more than one place, for more than one function.

alternative furniture arrangements: other functional ways to arrange the same furniture in the same room for variety, interest, and adaptability to the needs of the family.

condominium: a multiunit structure, such as an apartment house, in which each unit is individually owned (pages 42–43).

"fill-in" furniture: inexpensive furniture that serves an intended purpose temporarily until better quality pieces can be afforded.

flexible planning: furniture-arrangement planning which provides practical and useful alternative furniture arrangements.

living zones: areas of a home in which specific activities, such as reading, television viewing, meal preparation, or conversational exchange, take place.

townhome: a type of condominium that can be rented or jointly owned.

"visually" dividing space: separating one area of a room from another within the same room to create specific living zones; can be achieved by the appropriate placement of a folding screen, sofa, bookcase, or area rug.

STUDY ACTIVITIES

Required Activities

1. Using the floor plans given in your student packet, complete assignment two on

page 286 in your text. If possible, photocopy these floor plans and templates, since they will be used again in other assignments.

2. Select one wall from the floor plans in the student packet, complete a scale drawing of the wall elevation, and create a storage unit that is functional and attractive. Include storage space for books, pictures, games, television, one or two pieces of sculpture, and provide some interesting lighting.

Extra-Credit Activities

1. Review the checklist for arranging furniture on page 288 of the text, and study the room illustrated in Figure 10.1 (text page 267). Write a one-to-two-page paper analyzing and evaluating this room according to the checklist.

2. Use graph paper and furniture templates to develop two alternate furniture arrangements for the living-dining area of a small condominium. The area you are to use is a 15′ x 20′ rectangle. Assume the owner is a writer and needs work space at home, has a seven-year-old child, and belongs to a group of eight people who meet once a month, in members' homes, for dinner and book discussion.

STUDY QUESTIONS

(Select the one best answer.)

Comprehension Objective 1:   Describe the limitations and challenges of designing furniture arrangements for small-scaled dwellings.

1. The living zones in a mobile home or apartment may need to be "visually" established by
   a. a furniture grouping.
   b. a folding screen.
   c. an area rug.
   d. any or all of the above devices.

2. According to the designer in the television program, overscaled furniture in a small room can actually make the room look larger.
   a. true
   b. false

3. When designing a multi-use living room plan for a small-scaled dwelling, it is important to
   a. include two hide-a-bed sofas for overnight guests.
   b. realize traffic patterns will not be important due to the smaller amount of available space.
   c. include a variety of chairs in both large and small scale.
   d. assess the family needs, list the activities, and establish traffic paths before dividing the room into areas.

Comprehension Objective 2:   Explain the importance of and techniques for developing adaptable furnishing plans for mobile life styles.

4. Furnishings for an owner with a mobile life style who lives in a small-scaled dwelling should
   a. be adaptable.
   b. be neutral in color.
   c. be small scale.
   d. meet all of the above requirements.
   e. be all of one period or style.

5. To be adaptable, furniture should have
   a. a modular look.
   b. a low price.
   c. transitional colors.
   d. more than one use.
   e. all of the above qualities.

6. Which would be the best seating choice for someone with a mobile life style?
   a. several modular pieces
   b. a 9-foot sofa in a neutral color
   c. three or four chairs of varying scale and style
   d. one sofa and two matching chairs

Comprehension Objective 3:   Cite five ideas that may be incorporated into a flexible, low-cost interior design plan.

7. When working with a limited budget the best guideline to follow is to
   a. invest in slipcovers rather than reupholstering.
   b. paint the walls instead of wallpapering.
   c. make certain what you buy is of good quality.
   d. avoid decorating "fads."
   e. do all of the above.

8. The best advice for purchasing "fill-in" furniture is to
   a. buy the most expensive you can afford.
   b. indulge yourself in something "trendy" since you will not be keeping it long.
   c. look for items that will serve several functions.
   d. avoid purchasing "fill-ins" and wait to buy what you really want.

9. Which of the following are examples of "fill-in" furniture?
   a. armoires, bookcases, or shelves that cover a large wall
   b. lamps, pillows, or other accessories
   c. a bed, table and chairs, or a sofa
   d. canvas captain's chairs suitable for either dining or occasional seating

10. When planning your furnishings budget the first priority should be
    a. one or two outstanding accessories.
    b. furnishings that provide comfort and convenience.
    c. a washer and dryer.
    d. a table and chairs.

ANSWER KEY

(Page numbers refer to your text.)

1. d (study guide)
2. a (television program)
3. d (television program)
4. d (television program)
5. d (television program)

6. a (page 275)
7. e (television program)
8. c (television program)
9. d (study guide)
10. b (study guide, television program)

BENEATH YOUR FEET

OVERVIEW

A revival of **hard-surface flooring** has swept through the country during the past twenty years. This revival can be at least partially attributed to the new, easy-care materials now on the market and the improved qualities of old ones. Today most residential interiors include at least one type of **resilient, nonresilient**, or wood floor covering.

Floors contribute to the expressive character of an entire house. They can define and separate areas, suggest traffic patterns, and be as dominant or unobtrusive as desired. An undemanding, plain surface can be a passive yet unifying base for furniture; a bold pattern can call attention to the floor and establish the theme for a living space. In short, space planning can be intensified through the creative use of floor materials.

The overwhelming variety of types, colors, textures, and patterns of floor coverings can make it difficult to find the perfect floor covering if you do not have at least a slight idea of the functional and esthetic qualities your floor covering should have. The selections of resilient, nonresilient, and wood floorings should be based on evaluations of the product's functional characteristics, maintenance requirements, and aesthetic qualities in relation to overall cost. Some points to consider before purchasing a particular covering might be the character and beauty of the floor-covering material itself, the effect of the covering in the area for which it is being considered, and the relation of all of the floors in the home to one another and to the design of the entire house.

During your examination of floor materials, keep in mind the interrelationship of color, texture, and pattern. When applied to coverings, these elements should suggest the function; in other words, the floor should look as if it were meant to be walked on.

Some important factors to consider when choosing suitable floor coverings for your home would be durability, resiliency, and economy of upkeep. For example, floor materials that resist stains and bleaches or do not absorb liquids and dirt are easier to maintain than others. Additional factors include warmth, sound absorption, light reflection, and, of course, appearance. Try to insure that the flooring you eventually choose is comfortable as well as attractive and practical. For example, a **wood parquet** floor with a wire brush finish may look beautiful and help emphasize the mood or theme of a room, but it would provide little comfort for bare feet.

Although most people evaluate floor coverings in very small samples and at close range, the effect given by large areas and viewing from a distance in the perception of any design should not be overlooked. Some patterns, when repeated over a large area, become overwhelming. In contrast, some small repeat patterns tend to blend together and create the illusion of texture rather than pattern. The effect of color in a small pattern can also be changed when this blending occurs.

Your text offers solutions to design problems that might arise in choosing hard-surface flooring. It emphasizes the use of particular materials to achieve themes and moods, the suitability of material to the function of a room or area, the initial cost, and the cost of maintenance. Refer to the table on pages 165–169 of your text for a comprehensive, descriptive guide to hard-surface flooring.

No one flooring material is perfect in every respect, so it makes sense to decide which factors are most important to you and which compromises are necessary when selecting suitable floor coverings for your home.

LEARNING OBJECTIVES

After reading the assignment, viewing the program, and completing the assigned activities, you will be able to accomplish the following objectives:

Comprehension Objectives

1. Describe the functional and maintenance characteristics of four specified hard-surface floor coverings.
2. Cite two advantages and two disadvantages for both nonresilient and resilient floor coverings.
3. Identify the characteristics of sheet vinyl and cushioned no-wax sheet vinyl.
4. Analyze the effect of plastic impregnation on wood flooring.

Skill Objectives

1. Select three different types of wood flooring and suggest an appropriate room theme or mood for each type.
2. Given a house plan, select floor coverings for each room to provide for ease of maintenance, function, economy of resources, and desired esthetic qualities.

ASSIGNMENTS

Before Viewing the Program

□ Read pages 163–173 in the text, noting particularly those terms listed in the glossary in this lesson.
□ Read the comprehension and skill objectives for this lesson in the study guide.
□ Carefully study the overview, highlighting the important points and new concepts.
□ Look over the study activities and study questions for this lesson.

View the Program "Beneath Your Feet"

While viewing the program, note specifically:

□ the three most popular resilient or nonresilient floor coverings in use today, and the characteristics of each.

□ the advantages and disadvantages of vinyl flooring, tile or stone flooring, and wood flooring.

□ Differences in installation procedures for floors that are professionally installed versus those you can install yourself.

After Viewing the Program

□ Review the glossary terms and learning objectives.

□ Complete the study activities.

□ Test your understanding of this lesson by answering the study questions at the end of the lesson. Check your answers with the key.

GLOSSARY

(Page numbers refer to your text.)

acrylic wood flooring, page 172

ceramic tile, page 166

hard-surface flooring, page 163

nonresilient flooring, page 163

plastic-impregnated wood, page 172

quarry tile, page 165

random plank, page 170

resilient flooring, page 163

sheet vinyl, page 169

terra-cotta, page 165

vinyl tile, page 169

wood parquet, page 170

wood veneer, page 170

STUDY ACTIVITIES

Required Activities

1. Visit a local retail outlet that features a variety of hard-surface flooring. Compare types of hard-surface floor coverings with regard to aesthetic and functional properties as well as cost. Write a one-to-two-page paper describing your findings.

2. Add a section of hard-surface floor coverings to your resource file of interior design ideas. You may want to use brochures collected from retail stores. Select several types of flooring and label specific characteristics that you find attractive.

Extra-Credit Activities

1. Select a hard-surface floor covering that would be suitable in establishing an informal,

country mood. Write a one-to-two-page paper describing the flooring and listing its desirable surface characteristics.

2. Select a ceramic tile pattern and arrange a scheme that would be compatible with an existing resilient floor covering or soft floor covering. Write a one-to-two-page paper describing the tile, the mood that will result, and the advantages and disadvantages of ceramic tile.

STUDY QUESTIONS

(Select the one best answer.)

Comprehension Objective 1: Describe the functional and maintenance characteristics of four specified hard-surface floor coverings.

1. Which of the following floor coverings would *not* be a good choice for absorbing and storing solar energy?
   a. concrete tile
   b. brick
   c. exposed aggregate
   d. glass tile
   e. quarry tile

2. The advantage ceramic tile offers over asphalt, leather, rubber, cork, or glass tile is that it
   a. resists grease stains.
   b. cannot be damaged by heat or flame.
   c. collects and stores solar heat.
   d. is impervious to chemical stains.
   e. has all of the above qualities.

3. According to your text, the most versatile and widely used flooring material is
   a. ceramic tile.
   b. vinyl tile.
   c. wood.
   d. brick.

4. You are selecting a flooring for a gentleman's study, and he prefers a quiet, formal, elegant look. Which flooring choice below would best meet that standard?
   a. marble
   b. rough-sawn wood parquet
   c. slate
   d. leather tile

Comprehension Objective 2: Cite two advantages and two disadvantages for both nonresilient and resilient floor coverings.

5. A resilient floor covering offers
   a. greater comfort underfoot.
   b. easier installation.
   c. lower initial cost.
   d. all of the above advantages.

6. Your primary concern is to select a hard-surfaced floor covering with the capacity to store solar energy. Which type should you choose?
   a. resilient
   b. nonresilient

7. Which quality is *not* considered to be an advantage of nonresilient floorings as opposed to resilient floorings?
   a. easier maintenance
   b. longer usage
   c. lower installation costs
   d. greater durability

Comprehension Objective 3:   Identify the characteristics of sheet vinyl and cushioned no-wax sheet vinyl.

8. Identify the hard-surface flooring that is most resilient underfoot, has a protective vinyl coating, and is easy to maintain due to its nonporous surface.
   a. sheet vinyl
   b. poured seamless vinyl
   c. asphalt tile
   d. leather tile

9. If comfort underfoot were your primary concern, which of the following would be the best choice for a hard-surfaced kitchen flooring?
   a. cushion-backed vinyl
   b. kitchen carpeting
   c. cork tiles
   d. linoleum

Comprehension Objective 4:   Analyze the effect of plastic impregnation on wood flooring.

10. The main advantage of plastic impregnated wood flooring over other types of wood floors is its
    a. lower cost.
    b. increased durability.
    c. wider range of colors.
    d. beautiful patina.

11. The best choice for a low-maintenance wood flooring in the kitchen would be
    a. stenciled wood.
    b. stained wood.
    c. wood veneer.
    d. plastic impregnated wood.

ANSWER KEY

(Page numbers refer to your text.)

1. d (page 166)
2. e (pages 165, 166, and 168)
3. c (page 170)
4. d (page 169, television program)
5. d (page 163)
6. b (page 165)

7. c (page 163, television program)
8. a (page 169, television program)
9. a (pages 168–169)
10. b (page 172)
11. d (page 172)

TREAD
SOFTLY

OVERVIEW

Throughout history, people have covered the hard floors of their homes with various types of softer coverings in order to provide warmth, beauty, and comfort. Soft floor coverings are used today, too, for those same purposes. They also are used to unify rooms, create an illusion of spaciousness, or lend a feeling of closeness or intimacy.

The careful choice of a soft floor covering can add definite characteristics to a living space. The size, color, texture, and pattern of the covering can affect the style of a room. Even the amount of floor covered can emphasize a desired mood or theme, as well as increase or decrease the apparent size of a room. For example, if you are trying to achieve a feeling of spaciousness, choose a light, solid-color, wall-to-wall carpeting. If it is extended throughout adjoining areas, that same wall-to-wall carpeting will create a look of unity.

Rugs and **carpets** are distinguished by size. Rugs come in precut, specific sizes and shapes, have finished edges, and can be moved easily. Carpets are made by the yard and are usually permanent installations. A room-sized rug can create the effect of wall-to-wall carpeting, but because it is not tacked down, it is more practical for people who move often.

The fibers most commonly used for soft floor coverings are **nylon, acrylic, polyester, olefin,** and **wool**. For special purposes, silk, grass, rush, cotton, and other plant fibers such as sisal, jute, and even strips of paper are sometimes used. At one time, wool was the major carpet and rug fiber, but the popularity of manmade fibers, the diminishing sources of good carpet wools, and the resulting high cost of wool has led to a decline in wool usage. Nylon is now the predominant carpet fiber, followed by acrylics, polyesters, and olefins.

Four major methods of constructing a machine-made carpet or rug are **tufting, weaving, knitting,** and **needlepunching**. (Review the construction methods explained in pages 174–176 in your text.) Although more emphasis is placed on the fiber content and brand name of a carpet than on its construction, consumer knowledge of carpet and rug construction can facilitate the best selection.

Handmade rugs include the beautiful Oriental rugs from the Orient or Near East as well as folk, ethnic, or peasant rugs. Some of the first people to make rugs were shepherds and nomads, and modern methods of weaving with power looms are based on the ancient hand methods. Machine-made rugs that resemble the genuine handmade Oriental rug are constructed on powered

Jacquard looms and are called domestic or American Orientals. They must be clearly labeled to distinguish them from the genuine Oriental rugs.

The texture and design of soft floor coverings are created during construction by varying the color and types of yarn used or by using a pattern attachment. After the floor covering has been constructed, the pattern, design, and texture can be changed by printing, carving, or sculpting the surface. In addition, settings can be varied on the tufting machine so that the carpeting can be made with both cut **pile** and uncut loop pile for a wide range of design effects. The amount of **twist** and the length and **density** of the pile also dictate the carpet style, durability, and its eventual use.

When selecting a rug or carpeting, essential product information can help in determining quality. This information includes the country of origin, the manufacturer's name, the generic names of the face fibers, cleaning instructions, and special finishes such as mothproofing or antistatic treatment. Also, all carpets now on the market must pass a government test for flame retardancy.

You should also "use your hands and eyes" to evaluate the quality of a carpet. The television program for this lesson demonstrates some evaluation pointers: the **"bottoms out"** test and fanning out the carpet fibers to check for strength and density, and checking the "twistability" of the fiber.

Once installed, a **carpet underlay** or "use cushion" will increase durability, make it easier to vacuum dirt from the flooring, and make the carpet a more pleasant walking surface. The text gives excellent information about the various types available and stresses that the quality of the underlay is of equal importance with the quality of the carpet.

Carpet manufacturers recommend that rugs and carpets be vacuumed twice a week in most areas and daily in areas that receive heavy traffic. Spots and stains should be removed immediately. If information on stain removal is not included on the label and is unavailable from the source of purchase, you can write the Carpet and Rug Institute in Dalton, Georgia, and ask for a copy of the booklet, "How to Care for Your Carpets and Rugs."

Whatever type of carpeting or rug you choose, plan carefully and early to secure the effect and quality suited to your specific purpose. Make sure that your carpet or rug is an integral element in your interior design plan, one that complements the overall design of your home.

LEARNING OBJECTIVES

After reading the assignment, viewing the program, and completing the assigned activities, you will be able to accomplish the following objectives:

Comprehension Objectives

1. List two possible reasons for selecting each of the following types of soft surface floor coverings: wall-to-wall carpet, room-sized or large rugs, small area or accent rugs.
2. Cite at least three functions of carpet underlay.
3. Identify the factors used to evaluate the quality, construction, and texture of carpeting.
4. Evaluate the advantages and disadvantages of each of the following types of carpet fiber: wool, nylon, acrylic, polyester, olefin.

Skill Objective

1. Given examples of machine-made broadloom carpeting and handmade rugs, compare the specific features of each.

ASSIGNMENTS

Before Viewing the Program

□ Read pages 173–191 in the text, noting particularly those terms listed in the glossary in this lesson.
□ Read the comprehension and skill objectives for this lesson in the study guide.
□ Carefully study the overview, highlighting the important points and new concepts.
□ Look over the study activities and study questions for this lesson.

View the Program "Tread Softly"

While viewing the program, note specifically:

□ the basic manufacturing process involved in constructing broadloom carpeting as shown in the sequence in the carpet mill.
□ how designs are created for both machine and custom carpets.
□ how to check for quality in carpeting.
□ factors to consider when choosing from among various carpet fibers and constructions.
□ suggestions for care and cleaning of carpets and rugs.

After Viewing the Program

□ Review the glossary terms and learning objectives.
□ Complete the study activities.
□ Test your understanding of this lesson by answering the study questions at the end of the lesson. Check your answers with the key.

GLOSSARY

(Page numbers refer to your text.)

acrylic, page 174

"bottoms out":   a test for evaluating carpet density and thus quality. The test is accomplished by squeezing the carpet between the thumb and forefinger to see how easy it is to reach the carpet backing; the greater the density, the better the carpet.

carpet, page 179

carpet underlay, page 179

Kirman, page 184

nylon, page 174

olefin, page 174

STUDY ACTIVITIES

Required Activities

1. Using periodicals or catalogs, select two soft floor coverings, one with a formal mood and the other informal. Write a one-to-two-page commentary in which you suggest a suitable room for each covering and describe the type of furnishings appropriate to carry out the mood of each floor covering. Include comments on furniture details, color, and design features.

2. Visit a carpeting store with a stock of both machine-made broadloom carpeting and handmade rugs. If you cannot find a store that carries both, visit two appropriate stores. Carefully examine—"with the eyes and hands"—the construction, design, and quality of the two types of soft floor covering. Choose one covering from each category and write a two-page paper describing your findings.

Extra-Credit Activities

1. Compare the aesthetic and functional properties of various soft floor covering fibers by making a carpet and rug analysis chart. The following headings are suggested:

Fiber and Properties	Area Where Used	Advantages Disadvantages	Construction	Pile/ Density	Care/ Maintenance

When you make your chart, be sure to perform the following tasks:
   a. List properties of each carpet fiber and suggest uses. (What are the advantages and disadvantages of each fiber?)
   b. Describe the most appropriate construction techniques for the fiber and its intended use.
   c. Indicate pile height and density that would be most suitable for a particular fiber and area.
   d. Give suggestions for appropriate cleaning and maintenance.

2. Write a one-to-two-page paper explaining how a knowledgeable consumer can insure satisfaction when selecting carpeting.

STUDY QUESTIONS

(Select the one best answer.)

Comprehension Objective 1:   List two possible reasons for selecting each of the following types of soft surface floor coverings: wall-to-wall carpet, room-sized or large rugs, small area or accent rugs.

1. A light-colored, wall-to-wall carpeting used throughout a home will have which of the following effects?
   a. unifying the home
   b. providing color transition from room to room
   c. giving a more spacious appearance
   d. doing all of the above

2. Room-sized rugs have many of the advantages of wall-to-wall carpeting, plus the added feature(s) that they
   a. can be removed for cleaning.
   b. need no padding beneath the rug, thus greatly reducing the initial cost.
   c. can be turned to change the patterns of wear.
   d. have all of the above advantages.
   e. have the advantages described in a and c.

3. Technically, a carpet and a rug are the same.
   a. true
   b. false

Comprehension Objective 2:   Cite at least three functions of carpet underlay.

4. The advantage(s) of using a carpet underlay is (are)
   a. increasing carpet resiliency and wear.
   b. reducing pile matting.
   c. absorbing noise.
   d. creating a feeling of luxury
   e. described by all of the above statements.

5. Which of the following materials is *not* suitable as a rug or carpeting underlay?
   a. solid foam urethane
   b. waffle sponge rubber
   c. woven dhurri
   d. bonded foam urethane

Comprehension Objective 3:   Identify the factors used to evaluate the quality, construction, and texture of carpeting.

6. Which of the following is *not* considered an indicator of carpet quality?
   a. type and grade of fiber
   b. depth of pile
   c. density of pile
   d. cost
   e. construction

7. The most common method of carpet construction in use today is
   a. tufting.
   b. weaving.
   c. knitting.
   d. flocking.

Match the carpet surface textures on the right with the descriptions on the left by writing the corresponding letters in the blanks provided. Answers can be used more than once.

————	8. appropriate for more formal rooms	a.	level loop pile
————	9. usually found in tweed carpets	b.	cut or plush pile
————	10. once popular, now almost obsolete	c.	multilevel loop
————	11. has upright loops cut to form an even surface	d.	embossed
————	12. has characteristics of both shag and plush	e.	shag
————	13. generally made from nylon or olefin	f.	splush
————	14. versatile, available in wide price range		

Comprehension Objective 4:   Evaluate the advantages and disadvantages of each of the following types of carpet fiber: wool, nylon, acrylic, polyester, olefin.

15. The synthetic fiber most susceptible to pilling in carpeting or rugs is
   a. nylon.
   b. acrylic.
   c. polyester.
   d. olefin.
   e. source.

16. Which of the following carpet fibers best combines the qualities of resiliency, durability, soil resistance, and ability to accept dyes and clean well?
   a. nylon
   b. polyester
   c. wool
   d. olefin

17. The carpet fiber exhibiting the greatest number of desirable characteristics at an affordable cost is
   a. acrylic.
   b. wool.
   c. nylon.
   d. polyester.
   e. source.

18. Olefin fibers have many qualities that are also found in nylon. However, one important exception to consider is that olefin
   a. colors can have a dusty appearance.
   b. fibers are more difficult to clean.
   c. fibers are completely colorfast.
   d. is more appropriate than nylon for formal rooms.

19. The fiber that most resembles wool in appearance is
   a. nylon.
   b. source.
   c. acrylic.
   d. olefin.
   e. polyester.

20. Which of the following properties is *not* typical of polyester fibers?
    a. good abrasion resistance
    b. good stain and soil resistance
    c. easy to clean
    d. excellent resistance to crushing and pilling

ANSWER KEY

(Page numbers refer to your text.)

 1. d (page 179, television program)
 2. e (page 179)
 3. b (page 179)
 4. e (page 181)
 5. c (page 181)
 6. d (page 173)
 7. b (page 174)
 8. b (page 176, television program)
 9. c (page 176)
10. e (page 176)

11. b (page 176, television program)
12. f (page 176, television program)
13. a (page 175)
14. d (page 176)
15. b (page 174)
16. c (page 174)
17. c (page 174)
18. a (page 174)
19. c (page 174)
20. d (page 174)

FROM FIBER TO FABRIC

OVERVIEW

Often a consumer will select a beautiful **fabric** for use as window treatment, upholstery goods, household linen, or an accessory but give little or no attention to the fabric's functional qualities. Whether or not a fabric is durable or easy to maintain usually influences a homeowner's long-term satisfaction with that textile.

This lesson will help you to determine and evaluate the functional qualities of fabrics used as window treatments and upholstery materials. (This same consumer information can be used when evaluating textiles for other uses in an interior environment.) When it is time to make your fabric selection, it is essential that you know how to interpret information on labels, learn to evaluate quality, and ask retailers appropriate questions.

Because there is no fabric that works perfectly in all situations, your evaluations should always be made in relation to the product's intended use. For example, a fabric that functions beautifully as a window treatment is often inappropriate for use as upholstery. Some fabrics, though, are highly serviceable for both functions.

Your text discusses the primary characteristics and uses for the most common **fibers** found among interior textile selections. The table on pages 142–143 provides a good analysis of important properties of **man-made fibers**.

When evaluating the functional qualities of fabrics, consider the fiber content, type of construction, and any **functional** or **decorative** finishes that have been applied. The manufacturer's label will provide valuable information. For example, man-made fibers will be listed on the label by **generic names** (such as polyester, acetate, or rayon) and the manufacturer's registered **trade name** for the specific fibers also may be noted. For example, Dacron is a manufacturer's trade name for a polyester fiber. When a fabric is a blend of several fibers, each fiber imparts its own special functional and esthetic characteristics. Combining polyester with cotton, for instance, produces a fabric that has the esthetic qualities of natural cotton and the strength, wrinkle resistance, and ease of maintenance characteristic of polyester. The exact proportion of each type of fiber in the fabric is usually expressed in percentages.

The label will often list the fabric construction as well. Although there are many different processes by which fibers or yarns can be made into fabric, the usual method is weaving. The more common **weaves** are: plain, basket, twill, satin, tapestry, pile, and leno. Each type offers distinct esthetic and functional qualities. If the label does not provide this information, the construction of a fabric often can be determined by careful examination. The television program demonstrates ways to check for durability of the construction: the **test** for **dimensional stability** and holding the fabric up to the light.

Occasionally the manufacturer's label will provide information about chemical or mechanical processes used to add color or pattern to a fabric. The label also can include a manufacturer's guarantee pertaining to color permanency. When no printed information is provided, this aspect of fabric quality is perhaps the most difficult for the shopper to evaluate. Carefully inspect the individual fibers and yarns and the fabric back to determine the degree of color penetration. Complete color penetration through the fibers is extremely important in fabrics that will receive hard wear. A second simple test is to check for **color crocking** by rubbing the fabric surface against a lighter-colored fabric. If the lighter fabric picks up color, the fabric is likely to fade easily and to rub off on clothing.

Additionally, special finishes used to enhance a fabric's decorative and functional properties are often listed on the label by description or a registered trademark. The functional finishes usually have the greatest impact on consumer satisfaction. These include special processes that provide resistance to insects, mildew, shrinkage, wrinkling, fire, and soiling. In addition, antiseptic finishes reduce the likelihood of bacterial growth and absorption of odors. Antistatic finishes prevent the accumulation of static electricity.

However, a finish that adds one valuable characteristic can have certain disadvantages. For example, a finish added to increase the body and draping quality of a fabric may ultimately cause that fabric to change color or to yellow. Also, keep in mind that some finishes, such as those used to promote soil resistance, can be removed through normal cleaning processes and might not be replaceable.

As you evaluate the functional characteristics of a certain fiber content, construction, and finishing process, consider the desired esthetic qualities as well. Usually you will have to make value judgments based on the criteria most important to you and your family. These factors will be considered in Lesson Fifteen.

LEARNING OBJECTIVES

After reading the assignment, viewing the program, and completing the assigned activities, you will be able to accomplish the following objectives:

Comprehension Objectives

1. Identify the functional and esthetic characteristics of specific natural and man-made fibers. Explain how to evaluate those characteristics when planning fiber use for interiors.
2. Compare the characteristics of basket-weave and twill-weave fabrics and identify some uses for each.
3. Identify the functional and decorative finishes used on interior fabrics and discuss the importance of each as related to interior design.

Skill Objectives

1. Given a textile label, analyze the significance of all given information. Suggest additional information that would help the consumer make the best selection for intended use.
2. Given a sample of a printed fabric and label, explain how to evaluate the functional qualities of the fabric in relation to its fiber content, weave, print process, and finish.

ASSIGNMENTS

Before Viewing the Program

- □ Read pages 135–147 through the section "Lamp Shades" in the text, noting particularly those terms listed in the glossary in this lesson.
- □ Read the comprehension and skill objectives for this lesson in the study guide.
- □ Carefully study the overview, highlighting the important points and new concepts.
- □ Look over the study activities and study questions for this lesson.

View the Program "From Fiber to Fabric"

While viewing the program, note specifically:

- □ designer Peggie Collins describing the three qualities to consider when evaluating the suitability of a fabric.
- □ the physical properties of natural fibers as opposed to man-made fibers.
- □ fabrics and graphic drawings demonstrating various weaving methods and the discussion of how these methods influence the suitability and durability of a fabric.
- □ the test for "dimensional stability" of a fabric and the value of examining a fabric through light.
- □ the difference between patterns that are woven into fabrics and those that are applied.
- □ the information given on a manufacturer's label and how it helps consumers evaluate a fabric for an intended use.

After Viewing the Program

- □ Review the glossary terms and learning objectives.
- □ Complete the study activities.
- □ Test your understanding of this lesson by answering the study questions at the end of the lesson. Check your answers with the key.

GLOSSARY

(Page numbers refer to your text.)

bonding, page 140

crocking, page 155

decorative finishes, page 141

dimensional stability test: pulling the diagonally opposite corners of a square of fabric to determine whether the fabric would stretch or sag with time or wear.

dyeing processes: solution, stock, yarn, piece (see page 140)

fabric, page 135

felting, page 140

fiber, page 135

STUDY ACTIVITIES

Required Activities

1. Select two fabrics, one suitable for a window treatment, and the other for an upholstered chair. Write a two-page paper evaluating each fabric according to its intended use. Attach fabric samples to your paper.
2. Using an upholstered item in your own home or in a retail store, describe and evaluate the information on the upholstery fabric label. Determine the label's usefulness in defining the functional properties of the fabric. List additional information that would help in an evaluation of the fabric.

Extra-Credit Activities

1. List one functional and one esthetic characteristic for each of the following fibers: linen, cotton, nylon, polyester, acetate, acrylic.
2. Attach a sample of the following fabric weaves to a piece of poster board: plain weave, twill weave, satin weave, basket weave. Beside each fabric sample, write a brief description of the characteristics that would indicate its durability as an upholstery fabric.
3. Write a one-to-two-page paper discussing the importance of evaluating the fiber content, construction, and finishing processes of a fabric when determining its functional characteristics.
4. Name and describe three fabric finishes that would improve the functional qualities of an upholstered fabric.

STUDY QUESTIONS

(Select the one best answer.)

Comprehension Objective 1:   Identify the functional and esthetic characteristics of specific natural and man-made fibers. Explain how to evaluate those characteristics when planning fabric use for interiors.

1. Which of the following is a generic fiber name?
   a. arnel
   b. orlon
   c. nylon
   d. dynel
   e. acrilan

2. Identify the natural fiber listed below which is soft and luxurious, stronger than nylon, but can be damaged by direct sunlight.
   a. wool
   b. silk
   c. cotton
   d. flax
   e. ramie

3. Which is a mineral fiber best known for its fire retardant quality?
   a. nylon
   b. rayon
   c. asbestos
   d. cork

4. Wool fibers function well when used for household articles because they
   a. are resilient and resist abrasion.
   b. are easily dyed.
   c. are flame retardant.
   d. resist soiling and clean well.
   e. have all of the above qualities.

Comprehension Objective 2:   Compare the characteristics of basket-weave and twill-weave fabrics and identify some uses for each.

Match the types of weaves on the right to the illustrations on the left by writing the corresponding letters in the blanks provided.

a. plain weave

b. basket weave

c. twill weave

d. satin weave

e. leno weave

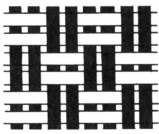

_____ 5.

_____ 6.

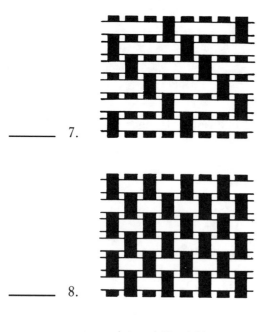

_____ 7.

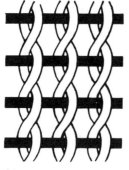

_____ 8.

_____ 9.

10. Select the fiber and construction method that would be best for an upholstered chair receiving heavy wear in a family room.
    a. acetate in a basket weave
    b. nylon in a twill weave
    c. polyester in a satin weave
    d. wool that is felted

Comprehension Objective 3:   Identify the functional and decorative finishes used on interior fabrics and discuss the importance of each as related to interior design.

11. Why would a roller-printed, acetate/nylon blend fabric be a poor choice for an unlined window covering?
    a. The colors would face too easily.
    b. It would be too expensive.
    c. It wouldn't drape well.
    d. It would require dry cleaning that is expensive.

12. Which of the following is *not* considered a finishing process?
    a. roller printing
    b. bleaching and shrinking
    c. mothproofing
    d. felting
    e. soil and water repellence

13. Printed designs can easily be distinguished from woven designs by
    a. feeling the direction of the nap.
    b. comparing the wrong side of the fabric to the right side.
    c. reading the manufacturer's label.
    d. doing all of the above.

ANSWER KEY

(Page numbers refer to your text.)

1. c (page 142)
2. b (page 136)
3. c (page 136)
4. e (page 136)
5. b (page 138)
6. d (page 138)
7. c (page 138)

8. a (page 138)
9. e (page 138)
10. b (pages 137, 142–143, television program)
11. a (page 142)
12. d (page 140, television program)
13. b (television program)

FINISHING WITH FABRIC

OVERVIEW

Stop and think just how dull and uninteresting most rooms would be without the use of fabrics. Fabrics are the most versatile and effective medium for incorporating texture, color, and pattern into a room's design. Although fabrics are most commonly used for upholstery and window treatments, your text describes selection criteria for other principal decorative uses. In addition to those listed, fabrics may be effectively used for accessories such as table covers, framed fabric "pictures," and pillows.

Because of the tremendous variety of types, colors, **textures**, and **patterns** of fabrics, you can usually find the "perfect" fabric for your tastes and needs. At the same time, however, the large selection may lead to confusion and frustration unless you know what characteristics you want. This lesson presents a number of guidelines for selecting fabrics.

Keep in mind the interrelationship of color, texture, and pattern when you are evaluating a fabric. For example, a blue color in a shiny, light-reflective fabric will usually appear lighter than will the same color in a coarse, nubby texture. And a large-scale pattern will often appear even larger and heaver if the color is intense rather than subdued.

Since light affects the appearance of color, all fabrics should be carefully evaluated in both the natural and the artificial light in which they will be seen within a specific room. When selecting sheer curtain or drapery fabric, be sure to allow the natural light to filter through the sample. You will then be able to determine if the color of the fabric, or even the light entering the room, is changed.

Although most people evaluate fabric at close range, the role that viewing at a distance plays in design perception should not be overlooked. If fabric is being selected for textural interest, remember that from a distance some textures become almost invisible. Small repeat patterns frequently blend together or into the background, creating an illusion of texture rather than pattern. In addition, such patterns can change the overall color of the fabric. When viewed from a distance, for example, a small blue-and-red check sometimes appears as a textural purple fabric.

All fabrics used within one room should relate to or even set the mood or theme of the room. Although this lesson will not identify all the fabric possibilities for various room themes, you will need to develop an awareness of colors, textures, and patterns that create or enhance specific themes or moods. Learn to identify some of the more common fabric types. Using descriptive adjectives for various fabrics, such as coarse, nubby, **informal**, **formal**, and elegant, can also be helpful when you select fabrics to express a consistent mood.

Contemporary fabrics frequently depend on color and texture for interest. When a pattern is incorporated, it is usually a geometric or abstract design. The degree of formality and informality may be determined by the specific color and type of textural interest selected. For example, a coarse homespun fabric in an earthy brown will "feel" more informal than a fine textural linen in a light blue—yet both could reflect a **contemporary** flavor. A few fabrics lend themselves to both contemporary and **traditional** themes. However, brocade, damask, silk, needlepoint, satin, and similar fabrics are usually more suitable for a formal, traditional look, while traditional informality is most often expressed with fabrics such as chintz, muslin, crewel, and printed and checked cottons.

When coordinating patterns to be used in one room, apply the principles of design and evaluate each pattern as it relates to the others and to the entire room. Your text provides excellent guidelines for selecting patterns to use singly or mixed with others in one room. When you are learning how to coordinate your selections, remember that (1) well-chosen geometrics can usually be combined with all other design types, (2) two geometrics can be used together, and (3) it is more difficult to create satisfactory combinations when you use two or more naturalistic or stylized designs within one room. Also, attempting to match a color in a patterned fabric can lead to a "too-decorated" look. A blend in color relationships offers the best results.

An interesting way to incorporate another pattern into a room's design is through the use of a "contrast welt." A **welt** is a strip of material sewn between upholstery seams to give a finished appearance. This piece of material usually has cording running through it and can be made of matching or contrasting fabric. When you visit a model home or a retail showroom, notice how contrast welting can be used to pick up certain colors in the design scheme or to enhance patterns used throughout the room.

After you have studied the available fabrics and narrowed your selections to a few, you may request **loan samples** and make the final decision in your own home. You will then be able to evaluate the fabric in relation to your lighting and to other fabrics in the room and check for color compatibility.

Be sure to ask for a loan sample cutting from the **current dyelot** of your fabric, as dyelots often differ to a subtle, and sometimes to a great, degree. For example, velvet-like fabrics from different dyelots often vary considerably in hue, value, or intensity from the original or loan sample.

When ordering your sample, be sure to **reserve** the number of yards you will need from the same dyelot. This temporarily holds the amount of yardage you need, preventing the problems that come with matching your fabric to that from another dyelot.

Your text includes several design problems that can be solved by well-considered fabric choices. In addition, understanding the importance of the elements and principles of design as applied to fabric selection will provide you with the ability to solve many other design problems. These guidelines will also help you to create the visual flow or transition throughout a home which is so essential to a unified design. Let the color, texture, or pattern relationships of the fabrics used from room to room help you achieve this cohesive design effect. Combining and coordinating fabrics for your home represents one of the greatest challenges in interior design, as well as one of the most enjoyable and exciting experiences.

LEARNING OBJECTIVES

After reading the assignment, viewing the program, and completing the assigned activities, you will be able to accomplish the following objectives:

Comprehension Objectives

1. Identify three uses for fabrics in interior design. List and explain the characteristics essential to fabrics selected for each use.
2. Cite the characteristics which determine whether a fabric is informal or formal.
3. Explain how fabrics can be used in a room to solve the following design problems: poor furniture balance, no established theme or mood, lack of harmony or unity in existing pieces.

Skill Objectives

1. Given a solid-colored upholstery fabric, select compatible fabric textures for the window treatment and for a second upholstered piece of furniture for one room.
2. Applying guidelines for mixing compatible patterns, select a fabric with a print design and describe in detail three other patterns that could be used individually with the identified fabric.
3. Using established criteria, develop a complete color and fabric plan for a room.

ASSIGNMENTS

Before Viewing the Program

- Read pages 145–159 in the text, noting particularly those terms listed in the glossary in this lesson.
- Read the comprehension and skill objectives for this lesson in the study guide.
- Carefully study the overview, highlighting the important points and new concepts.
- Look over the study activities and study questions for this lesson.

View the Program "Finishing with Fabric"

While viewing the program, note specifically:

- designer Sheri Miner displaying a variety of textures and patterns available in one predominating color.
- "no color scheme" fabric and how this basic fabric can be enhanced and accented with a variety of coordinating ethnic prints.
- fabric coordination "mistakes."
- how fabric changes the appearance of scale in three chairs of identical size.
- guidelines for coordinating fabrics to achieve a color scheme for a room and how this scheme can be used with variations throughout a home.
- the three "looks" fabric patterns can have and guidelines for combining patterns.

After Viewing the Program

- Review the glossary terms and learning objectives.
- Complete the study activities.
- Test your understanding of this lesson by answering the study questions at the end of the lesson. Check your answers with the key.

GLOSSARY

(Page numbers refer to your text.)

casement fabrics, page 155

color flag, page 155

colorline, page 155

contemporary fabric: textiles featuring geometric or abstract patterns as well as strong textural interest.

current dyelot: all of the fabric in a specific numbered dyebath. Numbered dyelots help the customer insure that fabric colors will match.

formal fabric, page 148

gimp, page 156

informal fabric, page 148

loan sample: one-fourth- or one-half-yard swatches of fabrics which are loaned to decorators or consumers so that they can check fabrics in the actual settings in which they will be used.

pattern, page 147

texture: the roughness or smoothness of a woven fabric as determined by the structure, weave, and thickness of the threads.

traditional fabrics;   fabrics which are at least slightly formal and which use stylized patterns, stripes, or small prints. Often traditional fabrics have floral patterns, but they can have checks, plaids, or a glazed finish.

reserve: a hold placed on fabric or carpeting to insure that all the yardage will be the same color when it is purchased.

welt, study guide overview

STUDY ACTIVITIES

Required Activity

1. Complete the assignment in your text on pages 158 and 159, using either Format 1 or Format 2.

Extra-Credit Activities

1. Name three qualities essential to satisfactory upholstery fabrics.
2. Choose and present to your instructor a sample of a bold floral print, as well as a second print to be used in the same room.
3. Write a one-to-two-page paper describing how fabric can be used to deemphasize furniture and windows.
4. Write a two-page paper explaining how fabrics can be used to create transitional flow throughout a home without creating monotony.

STUDY QUESTIONS

(Select the one best answer.)

Comprehension Objective 1:   Identify three uses for fabrics in interior design. List and explain the characteristics essential to fabrics selected for each use.

1. A satisfactory upholstery or slipcover fabric should
   a. be tightly woven.
   b. be durable.
   c. be easy to clean.
   d. have all of the above qualities.
   e. have the qualities described in b and c.

2. What additional characteristic(s) is (are) necessary for slipcover fabric but not as essential for upholstery fabric?
   a. is inexpensive
   b. does not require matching of patterns
   c. is pliable for easy fitting and sewing
   d. has all of the above qualities
   e. has the qualities described in a and c

3. A fabric selected for use as sheers, semisheers, or casements should
   a. be drapable.
   b. be sun-resistant.
   c. provide daytime or nighttime privacy.
   d. wash or clean well without shrinking.
   e. have all of the above qualities.

Comprehension Objective 2:   Cite the characteristics which determine whether a fabric is informal or formal.

4. Which of the following is *not* a typical characteristic of formal fabrics?
   a. high cost
   b. smooth textures
   c. stylized patterns or traditional stripes
   d. neutral colors

5. Informal fabrics are characterized by
   a. rougher textures than are used in formal fabrics.
   b. strong or contrasting colors.
   c. bold, naturalistic, abstract or geometric patterns.
   d. all of the above qualities.
   e. the qualities described in a and b.

6. Which of the following groups does *not* provide examples of formal fabrics?
   a. velvet or damask
   b. tweed or boucle
   c. satin or shantung
   d. brocade or taffeta

Comprehension Objective 3:   Explain how fabrics can be used in a room to solve the following design problems: poor furniture balance, no established theme or mood, lack of harmony or unity in existing pieces.

7. Repeating a small printed fabric on upholstery, lampshades, or draperies will help to achieve
    a. rhythm.
    b. unity.
    c. monotony.
    d. emphasis.

8. To increase the apparent size of a slightly undersized sofa, it would be best to cover it with a
    a. large pattern in a bold color.
    b. small pattern in a bold color.
    c. large pattern in a muted color.
    d. small pattern in a muted color.

9. A bold-patterned fabric used to upholster a small piece of furniture will
    a. create a new center of interest.
    b. have little effect on the apparent size of the chair.
    c. balance a larger piece of plain-colored furniture across the room.
    d. change the color scheme in a room

10. When combining patterned fabrics, it is easier to successfully incorporate two geometric designs than it is to use two naturalistic patterns.
    a. true
    b. false

ANSWER KEY

(Page numbers refer to your text.)

1. d (page 145)
2. c (page 145)
3. e (page 145)
4. a (page 148)
5. d (page 148, study guide)

6. b (page 148, study guide)
7. b (page 148
8. a (page 148)
9. c (page 148, television program)
10. a (study guide)

THE INS AND OUTS OF WINDOWS

OVERVIEW

Windows and their decorative covers or treatments are a versatile yet practical way to make a decorating statement. A window provides natural light, ventilation, and a certain amount of relief from the monotony of an unbroken wall. But it is the type of treatment that controls light and air and determines the visual appeal of the window. Window treatments can accent or eliminate a view, help establish the theme or mood of a room, provide insulation, and even reproportion an opening of awkward size or placement.

Before selecting an appropriate window treatment, the purpose and mechanical operation of the window must be carefully evaluated. Generally, windows are classified as **movable** or **fixed**. Within these two categories are many shapes, styles, and methods of opening. Windows that are movable and provide light, views, and climate control are probably the most familiar.

The window treatment and furniture arrangement should not interfere with the operation of the window. Double-hung windows have two frames that slide up and down, and swinging **casements** are hinged at one side and can swing in or out. Sliding casements move from side to side in horizontal sashes; thus they are easier to decorate and insulate than swinging casements.

Other types of windows present practical as well as decorative considerations. **Awning windows** are rather wide, horizontal panes of glass that swing out, as do the small paneled **jalousie** windows. Both types are very difficult to seal tightly, but they do offer good ventilation control. **Bay windows** and **bow bay windows** consist of three or more windows set at angles that project from the house to form an alcove. The **ranch**-style **window**, or horizontal **strip** of windows, is set high on the wall and consists of either sliding or swinging casements.

Fixed windows, which are less common than movable windows, supply only light and view. Dwellings with only this type of window must rely on expensive, mechanical ventilation systems. Examples of fixed windows are **skylights** (windows built into ceilings), **clerestories** (high, shallow windows), **arched windows** (with a series of curved panes at the top), and **picture windows** (those that have a large single pane of glass).

Usually those window treatments which enhance the architectural lines of the window are considered **architectural** or **structural**, and those treatments that soften and disguise the architecture are often referred to as **soft**. Either type of treatment can be constructed of textile or nontextile materials.

Although there are no set rules for the choice of window treatment, the design and styling of the fabric should be in keeping with the mood or theme of the room and should, of course, be based on the principles of design. Traditional and many formal settings call for opaque, sometimes heavy, fabric and elaborate borders and trims. This thematic treatment can be enhanced with tie-back overdrapes and an underdrape of some type. A more casual or country setting or theme may call for the homespun, natural look, small florals, or geometric designs. The more contemporary or modern mood calls for plain colors and streamlined treatments with texture as the main point of interest.

Curtains and **draperies** are two of the most common types of window treatments. Usually curtains are stationary and are made of sheer or light-weight fabrics. Draperies are made of heavier, sometimes opaque, fabric and can be either the stationary or the draw type. Draperies and curtains can be used alone or combined with other treatments, such as shades, blinds, shutters, or panels. Generally, curtains are considered to be less formal than draperies, but the texture, color, and pattern of the fabric greatly influence the ultimate look of the soft window treatment.

Draperies and curtains are constructed with a variety of **headings.** They may be shirred, pinch pleated, French pleated, box pleated, or made with tubular pleats ("cartridge construction"). These headings can be covered with borders, such as **valances, swags, cornices,** or **lambrequins.** Borders add interest, uniqueness, and variety to an otherwise simple treatment and can be used to emphasize the mood of the room.

When you choose a fabric for a window treatment, be familiar with the fiber qualities and the required care. Determine just how much natural light filters through your fabric, as it varies considerably from fabric to fabric.

Whether you decide to buy your curtains or draperies ready made, have them custom made, or make them yourself, it is essential that you measure your windows carefully. Follow these basic rules to insure that your measurements are accurate:

- Always take measurements with a steel tape measure or a carpenter's rule, since cloth tapes can stretch.
- Write down all the measurements of each window as you take them. Then recheck your measurements.
- Measure every window—even if some appear to be the same size.
- Measure the desired finished length of the window treatment. Floor-length curtains and draperies should barely clear the floor. For rooms with baseboard heat, choose a style and length that will not interfere with air flow.
- Measure the width of the treatment you plan. If it has a **return** (the distance between the rod and the wall), add that measurement to the width.

Today shades and blinds have assumed a much more important decorative role in treating windows. They offer practical solutions for light control, insulation, and energy conservation. There are three basic types of shades: roller (which is simple yet versatile, suitable for decoration), **Roman** (folds into horizontal which pleats when drawn), and **Austrian** (a formal elegant shade that folds in scallops or swages when drawn).

The standard **venetian blind** has been revitalized as a decorative treatment because of the variety of slat widths and colors now available. These blinds can be made from metal, wood, split bamboo, fabric laminate, woven wood, or a combination of these. They may be hung horizontally or vertically and can be custom made to specifications.

Shutters can be used in traditional as well as very contemporary settings. They are available with fixed and movable **louvers,** fabric panels, fretwork inserts, or custom designs. They can be painted, covered with fabric, wallpapered, or trimmed to suit the decor. And they can be used in combination with almost any other window treatment.

Some windows demand less treatment than others, and if privacy is not an issue, partial treatment or no treatment at all may be appropriate. By all means capitalize on a sensational view.

So many decisions are connected with developing an attractive interior window treatment that exterior window treatments are often overlooked as excellent remedies for heat control, ventilation problems, and light diffusion. Exterior treatments can provide these benefits without infringing upon the interior plans of a home. In fact, exterior window treatments can be used as the sole treatment or to complement those used inside. Therefore, exterior window treatments should be chosen with the same care that is used for the interior.

The most common exterior treatments are **awnings**, **shutters**, overhangs, grilles or fences, and louvers. Awnings made of weather-resistant fabrics or metal may be stationary or movable, allowing for easy adjustment. Today shutters are not as common as they once were, and they have evolved into fixed, decorative attachments. But when functional, shutters can provide insulation and also filter light. Overhanging roofs are popularly used in construction today to provide shade, to filter light, and as shelters for outdoor living spaces. Grilles or fences placed close to a window can offer privacy as well as sun and wind control.

If your budget allows, an antique or custom-stained glass window can provide a handsome focal point in a room. Indoor plants can also be arranged by a window to give partial coverage and create a dramatic effect when sunlight filters through the lush greenery.

No matter how you choose to treat the various windows in your room, try to unify the exterior and interior to maintain a consistent theme or mood.

Remember, too, the maintenance requirements and the durability of the treatment. Sometimes it is wise to invest in a more expensive treatment because it will require little maintenance or would be a permanent treatment for the life of the home.

LEARNING OBJECTIVES

After reading the assignment, viewing the program, and completing the assigned activities, you will be able to accomplish the following objectives:

Comprehension Objectives

1. Describe four types of window treatments commonly used by interior designers and explain the advantages of each.
2. Identify at least five specific criteria to use when selecting window treatments and explain how the application of each will help achieve functional and esthetic goals.
3. Describe two appropriate window treatments for both traditional and contemporary room settings.
4. Identify three characteristics indicative of quality construction in draperies and curtains.

Skill Objectives

1. Given window-treatment problems for a specific room, plan two window treatments that will correct the problems.
2. Cite examples showing when shutters, roller shades, or venetian blinds would be preferred window treatments rather than draperies or curtains.

ASSIGNMENTS

Before Viewing the Program

- □ Read pages 219–240 in the text, noting particularly those items listed in the glossary in this lesson.
- □ Read the comprehension and skill objectives for this lesson in the study guide.
- □ Carefully study the overview, highlighting the important points and new concepts.
- □ Look over the study activities and study questions for this lesson.

View the Program "The Ins and Outs of Windows"

While viewing the program, note specifically:

- □ the many ways windows and window treatments can enhance and improve the appearance of a room.
- □ how draperies are made and packaged for shipment in a drapery manufacturing company.
- □ Bob Passovoy, window treatment consultant, demonstrating how a basic drapery style can be varied with ties, fabric, and headings to produce different effects.
- □ quality and construction considerations in draperies, such as fabric stability, lining, and weighting.
- □ how to choose coordinating fabrics for sheers and draperies.
- □ sketches showing how to solve window problems.
- □ five factors to consider when selecting a window treatment.

After Viewing the Program

- □ Review the glossary terms and learning objectives.
- □ Complete the study activities.
- □ Test your understanding of this lesson by answering the study questions at the end of the lesson. Check your answers with the key.

GLOSSARY

(Page numbers refer to your text.)

apron, page 225

arched window, page 225

architectural or structural treatment: a window treatment which emphasizes the architectural design; can be achieved most commonly with lambrequins or cornices.

Austrian shade, page 236

awning window, pages 220–221

bay window, pages 222–223

bow bay window, pages 222–223

casement, pages 219–221

casing, page 225

clerestory, page 219

combination window, page 225

cornice, page 228

curtain: stationary window coverings that are usually made of sheer or light-weight fabrics.

dormer window, page 223

drapery: a stationary or draw type window covering constructed of relatively heavy fabrics and usually having a somewhat formal appearance.

fixed window, page 220

heading, page 227

jalousie, page 219

lambrequin, page 238

louvers, pages 220–221

movable window, page 220

picture window, page 222

ranch or strip windows, page 220

return, page 225

Roman shade, page 235

sash, pages 220, 225

sheers, page 230

shutters, page 231

sill, page 225

skylight, page 223

soft treatment: a window treatment of textile or other materials which disguises or softens the architectural shape, size, or design of a window.

stable drapery fabric: a fabric that will always maintain its dimensions.

stationary window, page 220

swag, page 228

valance, page 228

venetian blinds, page 234

window casing, page 225

window frame, 225

STUDY ACTIVITIES

Required Activities

1. Write a two-page paper evaluating the window types of each room in your home. Consider the direction of exposure and describe how the windows control ventilation, light, and heat.
2. Using a particular window in your home, design a window treatment that incorporates both architectural and soft-type treatments. Keeping in mind the theme of the room, list textures and patterns of all materials that would be used.

Extra-Credit Activities

1. Design treatments for the following "problem" windows"
   □ Windows located at different heights on the same wall.
   □ A pair of double-hung windows not centrally located on a wall.
   □ A series of windows placed above an architectural detail such as a radiator or heating vent.
2. Plan an exterior window treatment for one of the windows in your home. Explain why the treatment would be both functional and esthetically pleasing.

STUDY QUESTIONS

(Select the one best answer.)

Comprehension Objective 1:   Describe four types of window treatments commonly used by interior designers and explain the advantages of each.

1. Draperies differ from curtains primarily because they are movable and constructed of heavy fabrics.
   a. true
   b. false
2. Which of the following is *not* a benefit of using shades or blinds?
   a. They are more economical.
   b. They offer good light control.
   c. They provide insulation.
   d. They conserve energy.
3. You have a window with an unsightly view, yet you need to allow light into the room. Which of the following would be your best window treatment choice?
   a. miniblinds
   b. vertical blinds
   c. woven wood Roman shades
   d. roller shades
   e. a Shoji screen

Comprehension Objective 2:   Identify at least five specific criteria to use when selecting window treatments and explain how the application of each will help achieve functional and esthetic goals.

4. When selecting a window treatment, it is important to remember that the principal function of windows is to
   a. enhance the design plan.
   b. provide privacy.
   c. admit light and air.
   d. create a decorative focal point.
5. Which of the following is *not* a general classification of the types of windows found in homes today?
   a. movable
   b. decorative
   c. stationary
   d. combination

6. The primary considerations for selecting a window treatment should include
   a. the type of window and its placement in the room.
   b. the view outside the window and privacy requirements.
   c. the directional exposure and amount of light admitted.
   d. all of the above factors.
   e. the factors described in a and b.

Comprehension Objective 3:   Describe two appropriate window treatments for both traditional and contemporary room settings.

7. Other than the architectural style, which factor will have the strongest influence in determining whether a window will have a traditional or a contemporary theme?
   a. the location of the window
   b. whether the window is stationary or movable
   c. the type and color of fabric used
   d. how much energy control the window provides

8. Select the window style that would be most appropriate to a contemporary home.
   a. dormer window
   b. clerestory window wall
   c. french windows
   d. double-hung windows

9. Which of the following is *not* considered a contemporary window style?
   a. clerestory
   b. skylight
   c. greenhouse
   d. dormer

10. A traditional window treatment would use a fabric that
    a. is opaque rather than sheer.
    b. has a small floral or geometric print.
    c. has stripes or border trims.
    d. is described by any of the above phrases.

11. A nubby-textured, solid-colored, open-weave fabric would classify a window treatment as
    a. homespun.
    b. contemporary.
    c. structural.
    d. formal.

Comprehension Objective 4:   Identify three characteristics indicative of quality construction in draperies and curtains.

12. Lining functions best with drapery fabrics that are
    a. sheer and light-weight.
    b. loose and open weave.
    c. expensive and subject to sun damage.
    d. as described by all of the above phrases.
    e. as described by the phrases in a and b.

13. Weights are used in well-made curtains or draperies in order to
    a. hold the hem down on bulky fabrics.
    b. improve the way the fabric hangs.
    c. reduce sway caused by drafts.
    d. hold the corners in place.
    e. achieve all of the above goals.

ANSWER KEY

(Page numbers refer to your text.)

1. a (study guide)
2. a (page 234, study guide)
3. e (page 237)
4. c (page 219)
5. b (page 220)
6. d (page 220)
7. c (television program, study guide)

8. b (page 223)
9. d (page 223)
10. d (study guide)
11. b (study guide)
12. c (television program)
13. e (television program)

WHAT TO MAKE OF A WALL

OVERVIEW

Since walls occupy more space than any other single element in a room, they are an extremely important part of overall design. Today's technology has produced an unending variety of materials that add interest to walls.

Several factors should be considered before you decide on the wall covering or combination of wall coverings that will be used in a particular room. You should first determine the function of the room and the mood you want to establish. The scale of the walls is an important factor, one which affects the choice of intensity of patterns as well as color value. Consider, too, other furnishings within a room when selecting wall treatments. Furniture and wall-treatment choices should correspond in theme or mood, as well as color scheme. For instance, if your furnishings are traditional, you may want to choose wall treatments in patterns that are historical reproductions. If your furniture is sleek and modern, a brilliant wall graphic may be the appropriate selection.

Carefully planned wall treatments can emphasize or supplement the furnishings in a room. If you have a minimum of furnishings and accessories, a strong-patterned wall treatment can eliminate the need for pictures or wallhangings and tie together the limited furnishings. Conversely, walls can be an unobtrusive background for artwork and furniture. Also, your furniture arrangement might be complemented by making one wall a dramatic focal point and the others in the room more neutral. All of these effects are possible with wisely selected wall treatments.

Paint is a popular wall treatment because it can be applied easily, quickly, and inexpensively compared with other wall treatments. Painted walls are usually less obtrusive in a room scheme; however, paint can also be used for dramatic graphic effects and in combination with other materials for added emphasis.

The variety of available paints and colors can cause the consumer a great deal of confusion. Be sure to shop at reliable dealers and never hesitate to ask questions. Choose your paint according to the mood of the room, the use the room will receive, and the areas surrounding the walls to be painted.

Almost all paints can be divided into three basic categories: **solvent-thinned**, **water-thinned**, and **catalytic coatings**. Solvent-thinned paints are used mainly for exterior surfaces.

They dry slowly, have a strong smell, and must be thinned with turpentine or mineral spirits. Painting equipment must be cleaned with some type of solvent. If you do use this type of paint indoors, make sure the room is well ventilated during the painting.

Water-thinned paints can be used on interior or exterior surfaces. These paints dry quickly, and tools may be cleaned with water. This type of paint is referred to as **latex** and may be a composition of rubber, acrylic, and vinyl. Also included in this category are emulsion paints, which have the additional advantage of usually covering surfaces with one coat.

Catalytic paints, which are hardened by chemicals, provide the most durable finish. Although they can be used on most surfaces, they are not easy to apply. In addition, catalytic paints, including **epoxy**, urethane, or **polyurethane**, are expensive and emit irritating fumes.

Most paints are available in a variety of finishes, and it is important to consider finish when you are making your selection. Finishes include **flat**, **gloss**, **semigloss**, eggshell, and textured.

Flat paint should be used on walls that will receive minimum wear. Flat paint is easy to apply, can be wiped clean, and does not reflect light.

Enamels come in gloss, semigloss, and eggshell finishes. They provide excellent wear and should be used on surfaces that will need frequent scrubbing such as doors and moldings. Eggshell enamels, the least glossy, have been used traditionally in kitchens and bathrooms, but might also be a good choice for hallways.

If you have rough or damaged surfaces to cover, textured paints could be the solution. These paints either have a "sand" finish or resemble adobe or stucco. No matter what type of paint you use, read the labels carefully and obtain all necessary information and equipment before you begin.

With all of its versatility and ease of use, paint is not always the best wall treatment. If you need to provide additional insulation or acoustical qualities, or desire a more textured finish, another wall covering might be preferable. The rich look of wood adds to the esthetic quality of any room. Depending on the tone, texture, and quality of the wood used, wood can easily and attractively establish a mood of either formality or informality.

A variety of sizes and shapes are available in both precut and finished wood panels and squares. Wood may be installed alone or in combination with paint, wallpaper, or other wall coverings. Woods most commonly used are pine, walnut, redwood, birch, maple, and oak. For more choice in grain patterns and variation in tone, you can choose from teak, rosewood, and zebrawood. The price range for wood is wide, and if the wood is well chosen, wood can provide a lifetime of beauty and warmth with very little care.

Paint and wood, the two most versatile and popular wall treatments, can be an appropriate choice for any room. However, any wall-treatment selection should be based on the interrelationship of established needs, total cost, and, of course, the esthetic effect you wish to achieve.

LEARNING OBJECTIVES

After reading the assignment, viewing the program, and completing the assigned activities, you will be able to accomplish the following objectives:

Comprehension Objectives

1. Identify the factors that should be considered when selecting paint as a wall covering and the functional qualities of four types of paints.

2. Cite five factors to be considered when selecting wall treatments for a room.
3. Describe the general characteristics, appropriate uses, and visual effects of four popular wall coverings.

Skill Objectives

1. Plan and describe three "special-effect" wall treatments for three different rooms, using either paint or wood.
2. Using at least two values of one hue, illustrate a paint color scheme for a room. Describe the specific uses of each color value and explain the visual effect of the total plan.
3. Applying color selection criteria, select for three walls a paint color compatible with the wallpaper you have chosen for the fourth wall within a room.

ASSIGNMENTS

Before Viewing the Program

- Read pages 191–200 in the text, noting particularly those terms listed in the glossary in this lesson.
- Read the comprehension and skill objectives for this lesson in the study guide.
- Carefully study the overview, highlighting the most important points and new concepts.
- Look over the study activities and study questions for this lesson.

View the Program "What to Make of a Wall"

While viewing the program, note specifically:

- designer Carolyn Breeden describing factors to consider when selecting a wall finish.
- the reflective qualities of various colors.
- how wall colors affect the mood of a room.
- the appearance and use of four kinds of paint finishes.
- how to use paint chips to obtain a desired color.
- how to "test" a wall color and maintain a record of colors used.
- traditional and contemporary color schemes.
- the effects and application of wall graphics and stencils.
- textures, color values, and impact of wood used on walls.
- examples of wood used in combination with other wall treatments.

After Viewing the Program

- Review the glossary terms and learning objectives.
- Complete the study activities.
- Test your understanding of this lesson by answering the study questions at the end of the lesson. Check your answers with the key.

GLOSSARY

(Page numbers refer to your text.)

acoustical tile, page 200

acrylic paint, page 200

alkyd paint, page 200

catalytic paint: a chemically catalyzed epoxy paint which produces a hard, durable water- and mar-resistant finish.

enamel, page 200

epoxy paint, page 200

flat paint: an easy-to-apply paint with a low light reflective quality that can be wiped clean; not as durable as glossier finishes.

gloss: a shiny-surfaced paint finish which is easy to clean and reflects light.

latex, page 200

nonresilient wall coverings, page 196

polyurethane, page 200

semi-gloss: a paint finish with less surface shine and light reflection capacity than gloss but which is also easy to clean.

solvent-thinned paint: a chemically based alkyd paint which must be thinned with solvent or turpentine.

water-thinned paint: an acrylic paint that can be mixed with water for thinning purposes, that dries quickly, and that is easy to clean with water after painting.

STUDY ACTIVITIES

Required Activities

1. Create a file of at least ten interesting wall treatments that use paint, wood, or a combination of the two. Write a two-page paper briefly describing the feeling or effect of each treatment.
2. Visit a large paint store, compare the different types of paints, finishes, and the color ranges each offers. Gather a representative sampling of paint color chips and add to your resource file.

Extra-Credit Activity

1. Evaluate three rooms in your own home. To what extent does each wall treatment represent the mood you planned to create? If your room or rooms lack interest, choose a more compatible wall treatment that will enhance the overall scheme. Explain how wall treatments, furniture, and fabric styles work together to create a unified whole.

STUDY QUESTIONS

(Select the one best answer.)

Comprehension Objective 1:   Identify the factors that should be considered when selecting paint as a wall covering and the functional qualities of four types of paints.

1. When selecting paint for any room your primary consideration(s) should be
   a. the size of the house and the life style and budget of the family.
   b. your skills as a painter or handyman.
   c. the function of the room, theme or mood you wish to establish, and ease of maintenance.
   d. the color choices available and the geographic exposure.

2. Which of the following advantages do latex and acrylic paint offer over most other paints?
   a. They are fast drying and leave no overlap marks.
   b. They have no lingering odor or toxic fumes.
   c. They are easy to apply and clean up.
   d. They have all of the above advantages.
   e. They have the advantages described in b and c.

3. A suitable paint for the woodwork in a bathroom would be
   a. alkyd paint.
   b. latex enamel.
   c. enamel.
   d. any of the above.

4. The only paint durable enough for use in swimming pools or shower stalls is
   a. enamel.
   b. polyurethane.
   c. epoxy.
   d. lacquer.

5. The appearance of a paint color often changes when applied to a large area. To avoid such a change, choose a color
   a. two shades darker than the sample paint chips.
   b. two shades lighter than the sample paint chips.
   c. dilute with white paint to conteract the change.
   d. shaded with gray.

Comprehension Objective 2:   Cite five factors to be considered when selecting wall treatments for a room.

6. The most versatile wall treatment that can be used in any style room and with any style furniture is
   a. smooth plaster.
   b. brick.
   c. ceramic tile.
   d. glass block.
   e. solid wood.

7. A major drawback of applying plastic tiles or sheets is that they are
   a. available in only a few colors.
   b. a poor insulator with a low fire rating.
   c. difficult to keep clean.
   d. very susceptible to scratching.

8. If insulation qualities were the prime concern in selecting a wall treatment, which treatment below should be avoided?
   a. solid wood
   b. wallboard (gypsum)
   c. stone
   d. fiberglass panels
   e. glass blocks

Comprehension Objective 3:   Describe the general characteristics, appropriate uses, and visual effects of four popular wall coverings.

9. The safest guideline for selecting a paint color to coordinate with wallpaper is to
   a. select any color that appears in the wallpaper.
   b. choose the lightest neutral color in the wallpaper and match it.
   c. choose the darkest neutral color in the wallpaper and match it.
   d. match the paint with the wallpaper background.

10. The use of mirrors and mirror panels has increased in recent years due to
    a. the diminishing size of living spaces.
    b. their availability in large sheets and precut panels.
    c. their ability to "open up" small places and make a room appear larger.
    d. all of the above factors.

11. One of the few disadvantages of using wood as wall treatments throughout a home is that wood
    a. is difficult to keep polished.
    b. dents easily and cannot be repaired.
    c. is costly to install.
    d. has poor insulating qualities.

ANSWER KEY

(Page numbers refer to your text.)

1. c (study guide, television program)
2. d (page 200)
3. d (page 200)
4. c (page 200)
5. b (television program)
6. a (page 198)

7. b (page 198)
8. c (page 198)
9. d (television program)
10. d (page 195)
11. c (page 199)

DRESS THE WALLS

OVERVIEW

Papers and fabrics have been used to embellish interior dwelling surfaces for centuries. However, the popularity of these **resilient wall coverings** has increased during the last fifty years because of tremendous changes in design, fabrication, and application. Today's consumer has an overwhelming selection of patterns, colors, and material.

Selecting the appropriate resilient wall covering for an interior plan will be simple once you decide what you want the covering to contribute to your plan. The potential functional and esthetic contributions are: (1) color and pattern, (2) insulation, (3) sound absorption, (4) textural interest, (5) the capacity to esthetically integrate unrelated items, and (6) a camouflage for imperfection in the wall surface. These qualities combine to make wallpaper or wall fabric a valuable and versatile component in any design plan.

Some simple guidelines for selecting wall coverings were presented in the previous lesson. Additional guidelines should be applied for choosing wallpaper or fabrics. Today's wall coverings offer a wide selection of patterns and textures that blend with any style of furnishing. Look for a timeless pattern which provides a pleasant view, reflects the mood of your home, and has a surface which can be easily maintained.

Before you decide what type of wall covering you should use and the extent to which it will be used, assess the particular area. Wallpaper can hide some structural irregularities, but if the room or area is plagued by cracks, patches, or even holes, another material, such as wood paneling, might serve better. Pattern in wallpaper or fabric, however, can disguise many architectural irregularities, such as jogs, soffits, and even exposed conduits. If you are trying to conceal problems, a paper with an over-all pattern and random design would do the job best. Keep in mind, though, that the scale of a wall-covering pattern should relate to the size of the area in which it will be used. A very small pattern would become lost if used over a large expanse, and a bold, colorful pattern becomes even stronger when applied to walls.

Also, consider the design in relation to the theme or mood you wish to establish. There is a wall covering to blend or contrast with any style of furnishing. Designs currently available in wallpaper can be classified as **damasks, toiles, florals, geometrics, scenics or murals, almost naturals, metallic foils,** and **flocks.**

Damasks, which represent some of the oldest wall designs, are used most often in traditional room settings. Symmetrical fruits and flowers encased in curves are the usual motifs.

Toiles consist of stylized floral patterns or landscapes on a creamy background and are sometimes reproductions of eighteenth-century fabrics. These wall coverings fit well in traditional or period settings.

Florals encompass a wide category. They may be found in almost every color, style, and scale and can be chosen to establish many moods or themes.

Geometrics consist of any design based on straight lines, circles, or any combination of these and are appropriate in any room setting. For example, stripes work well in a traditional room, and any geometric style blends into an eclectic design. Checks look quaint and provincial in early American settings, while bold, large graphics add interest in modern design.

Scenic or mural papers have one large design meant to cover an entire wall. They can make areas look larger or can give a **trompe l'oeil** (three-dimensional) effect.

"Almost naturals" include simulated grass cloths and materials that look like leather, tile, or brick. Many of these papers are so effective that they almost look like the real thing.

Metallic foils usually have a paper backing, a thin layer of foil, and then a printed or flocked pattern, depending on the style. These papers are extremely fragile and may be damaged easily in both application and use.

Flocks are made by an electrostatic process. Synthetic fibers are attached to a paper backing to form the pattern and texture. Even if the background and flock are the same color, the contrast in textures gives a two-color appearance.

Wallpaper can be relatively inexpensive or very costly depending on the design or pattern, the number of colors, and additions such as vinyl coating, flocking, or fabric backing. Beyond the cost of materials, what you are paying for in expensive papers is the design and its exclusiveness. The most expensive wallpapers often represent the latest fashion in this industry.

Vinyl- and fabric-backed coverings are most commonly used today. They can be easily stripped off walls, and some can even be reused. The variations in vinyl wall coverings are: **vinyl-protected**, **vinyl latex**, **coated fabric**, and **plastic foam**. (See page 202 in your text.)

It is important that you notice the "run number" listed on a roll of wallpaper, and be sure that all the rolls you purchase of the same pattern have corresponding numbers. Colors often vary considerably from run to run.

If you want the special textures offered only by fabric, or want a wall to match a window treatment and no paper is available, fabric can be applied to your walls. The five ways to apply fabric are by using shirring, masking tape, Velcro, staples, and paste; all of these methods are described on pages 203–204 of your text. Note, however, that fabric is usually more expensive than wallpaper.

Fabric also demands special precautions in selection and installation. If you plan to attach fabric to a wall with glue or paste, be sure your fabric is thick enough so that the adhesive will not seep through. The fabric should also be resistant to stain, mildew, fading, and shrinkage. Some fabrics can be sprayed for increased stain resistance after they are applied. After the fabric is on the wall, you might want to apply some type of molding or trim at the top, the bottom, and the seams for a finished look.

LEARNING OBJECTIVES

After reading the assignment, viewing the program, and completing the assigned activities, you will be able to accomplish the following objectives:

Comprehension Objectives

1. Identify at least three different wallpaper design categories, suggest a room theme for each, and explain how the design would help to establish the identified theme.
2. Describe at least two flexible wall coverings and explain the functional and esthetic characteristics of each.

Skill Objectives

1. Evaluate two given wallpapers in relation to functional and esthetic characteristics for a small room.
2. Select three compatible wallpapers for use in three adjoining rooms that can be seen simultaneously.

ASSIGNMENTS

Before Viewing the Program

□ Read pages 201–208 in the text, noting particularly those items listed in the glossary in this lesson.
□ Read the comprehension and skill objectives for this lesson in the study guide.
□ Carefully study the overview, highlighting the important points and new concepts.
□ Look over the study activities and study questions for this lesson.

View the Program "Dress the Walls"

While viewing the program, note specifically:

□ designer Gil Roque discussing the esthetic and functional characteristics of wallpaper.
□ the types of wallpaper which are most likely to be "scrubbable," "washable," "strippable," or able to camouflage imperfections.
□ design features to be considered when selecting wallpaper.
□ the raised cylinder, rotogravure, and silk-screen methods of producing wall coverings.
□ samples of textural wall coverings.
□ suggestions for providing transition and coordination for wall coverings throughout a home.

After Viewing the Program

□ Review the glossary terms and learning objectives.
□ Complete the study activities.
□ Test your understanding of this lesson by answering the study questions at the end of the lesson. Check your answers with the key.

GLOSSARY

(Page numbers refer to your text.)

almost naturals, study guide overview

blank stock: special paper without color or design that is applied to a wall to cover imperfections.

chinoiserie, page 201

coated fabric, page 202

damasks, study guide overview

double or triple roll, page 203

flocked wallpaper, page 202, study guide overview

geometrics, study guide overview

hand blocking, page 202

metallic foils or mylars, study guide overview

plastic foam, page 202

prepasted, page 203

pretrimmed, page 202

resilient wall covering, page 201

roller printing, page 202

scenics or murals, study guide overview

scrubbable, page 202

silk-screen printing, page 202

single roll, page 203

toiles, study guide overview

trompe l'oeil, page 207 (This literally means "fool the eye.")

vinyl-protected wall covering, page 202

vinyl latex wall covering, page 202

washable, page 202

STUDY ACTIVITIES

Required Activities

1. Add to your interior-design resource file at least ten illustrations of wallpapers or fabrics. Explain how these illustrations represent functional and esthetic characteristics that you learned in this lesson.
2. Select three different wallpapers or fabrics to be used in three adjoining rooms that can be seen simultaneously. Explain why these treatments would be compatible.

Extra-Credit Activity

1. Evaluate two rooms in your home and select several samples of different wallpaper illustrating coordination between the rooms. Obtain paint chips showing the colors you could use and how various effects could be changed as the paint colors changed. Be certain to have your selections carry out your desired mood or theme.

STUDY QUESTIONS

(Select the one best answer.)

Comprehension Objective 1:   Identify at least three different wallpaper design categories, suggest a room theme for each, and explain how the design would help to establish the identified theme.

1. Which wallpaper style would be *unsuitable* for a home with a traditional theme?
   a. geometric mylar
   b. damask
   c. toile
   d. small floral
2. The *best* wallpaper choice for a compact-sized bathroom would be
   a. a dramatic geometric mylar.
   b. small-striped, prepasted paper.
   c. a vinyl-protected paper in a small pattern with a light background.
   d. a subtle striped, flocked wallpaper.
3. A natural, rustic, textured effect would best be expressed through the use of _____ wallpaper.
   a. damask
   b. grass cloth
   c. toile
   d. flocked stripe

Comprehension Objective 2:   Describe at least two flexible wall coverings and explain the functional and esthetic characteristics of each.

4. The primary consideration in selecting flexible wall coverings should be
   a. cost.
   b. flexibility.
   c. their ability to enhance or maintain the mood or theme throughout the home.
   d. current trends in decorating.
5. The wall covering that would be best suited for use in a kitchen is
   a. embossed wallpaper.
   b. vinyl-protected wall covering.
   c. silk-screened wallpaper.
   d. vinyl latex wall covering.
   e. plastic foam wall covering.

Match the wall coverings on the left with the corresponding descriptions of qualities on the right by writing the corresponding letters in the blanks provided. Answers can be used more than once, and some wall coverings will have more than one quality.

_____ 6. vinyl-protected	a.	scrubbable
_____ 7. vinyl latex	b.	washable, but not scrubbable
_____ 8. coated fabric	c.	strippable
_____ 9. plastic foam	d.	sound absorbable
_____ 10. cork	e.	soil resistant

ANSWER KEY

(Page numbers refer to your text.)

1. a (study guide)
2. b (study guide, television program)
3. b (television program)
4. c (study guide, television program)
5. d (page 202)

6. b (page 202, television program)
7. a, c (page 202, television program)
8. a, e (page 202, television program)
9. b, d, e (page 202, television program)
10. d (page 205)

WALL TO WALL

OVERVIEW

More than any other aspect of a room's design, walls as background areas serve to set the mood or theme. When subtle in color, texture, or pattern, they represent a supporting background for the other design components. When visually stimulating, because of intense colors, bold textures, reflective surfaces, and dramatic patterns, they command more attention and may even become a primary focal point in the room.

This lesson concentrates on how to make a good selection for a wall treatment to be used in any room. Although only a few different types of treatments could be shown in the program, the suggested guidelines can be applied to the selection of any type of wall treatment. Also shown is how to create a compatible mix of two or more wall treatments for one room.

Even though paint, wood, wallpaper, and fabric are the most commonly used wall treatment products, a wide variety of other materials can add interest to one or more walls in a room. **Architectural glass** in the form of mirrors is one of the most versatile of all wall treatments. Complete wall surfaces can be covered by mirrors, and the result is always a visual expansion in the size of the room. Even when architectural glass is used in small quantities in combination with other wall treatments such as wood or masonry, there is some visual expansion as well as increased design interest. Because of their reflective qualities, mirrors can double the impact of a good feature such as a crystal chandelier or a garden view. Before selecting mirrors for wall treatments, however, consider the following points: (1) good-quality mirrors are relatively expensive; (2) mirrors should be used only where the probability of breakage is minimal; (3) they must be meticulously clean to be attractive; and (4) they should be used where they will reflect desired images.

Other wall treatment products vary considerably in price and effect. Carpeting, for example can be quite costly and is not used extensively, but it does provide excellent sound absorption. It also adds textural interest and can be used to create unique graphic effects.

Plastics or other materials that imitate natural **masonry** products such as brick or stone are usually less expensive, easier for the homeowner to install, and more maintenance free than the original material. Although the purist often frowns on using such imitative materials, these products can provide a very attractive, serviceable wall covering when they are of a high quality.

There are other less commonly used wall-treatment materials—cork, tree bark, and leather tiles, for example—and new products will continue to appear on the market. As you expand your awareness of available products and learn interesting ways to use them in your designs, always keep in mind their cost, installation procedures, and required maintenance.

The most important point to keep in mind as you make your selections is that any wall treatment must relate to all other aspects of the room's total design. A brief review of Lessons Three, Four, and Five will help you insure successful results. Remember that all wall treatments should express the mood or theme and the degree of formality or informality indicated by the other design components. Although some variety should be introduced in the room, a harmonious relationship of colors, textures, and patterns is necessary. For example, coarse grasscloth would be an appropriate wall covering for many informal rooms, but in a formal setting a finer texture would be preferable.

How do you determine the degree of formality or informality in wall-treatment products? Generally, the most formal wall treatments are those that have reflective surfaces, very fine textures, light value and lower intensity colors, or a traditional pattern. Informality is expressed by nonreflective qualities, coarse textures, darker or more intense colors, or patterns depicting an informal subject matter.

Certain wall-treatment products can be used well in either very formal or informal designs. Depending on the other components in the room, nonpatterned ceramic tiles can be compatible in either a formal or an informal setting. Often the color, texture, and pattern determine the degree of formality of a wall covering. For example, rough-textured stucco walls are more rustic in mood than stucco walls that are smoothly finished.

Interesting design effects may be achieved by using different wall treatments on adjacent walls or by combining two or more treatments on one wall. Whether or not you choose to use more than one wall treatment will depend on the design effects you want and the size of the room. Usually, combining wall treatments will decrease the apparent size of the room. This illusion may be advantageous when you are attempting to visually change the dimensions of a room. If you choose more than one treatment in a room, however, one material should be visually dominant and should be used where emphasis is desired.

In the text assignment for this lesson, you will also learn of the design possibilities in various ceiling treatments. In contemporary homes, ceilings are often high to create a visual compensation for small rooms. Ceilings can also be lowered to create a feeling of intimacy. Treatments such as natural wood surfaces or beams and various tiling products can also be used on ceilings to provide textural interest and enhance the design and theme of a room. Ceiling and wall treatments, of course, should be compatible.

The compatibility of wall and ceiling treatments used in different rooms that can be seen simultaneously should also be considered. Although the rooms may be distinctly different, such as a living room and a bedroom, the surface treatments should not oppose or compete with one another. Good visual transition between the rooms in a home is a key factor in all of the components of design.

LEARNING OBJECTIVES

After reading the assignment, viewing the program, and completing the assigned activities, you will be able to accomplish the following objectives:

Comprehension Objectives

1. Identify at least three factors that should be considered when selecting a wall treatment for a room.

2. Identify techniques for planning wall treatments for one room in relation to treatments used in other rooms that may be viewed simultaneously.

3. Identify two types of ceiling materials and describe the contribution each makes to a room design plan.

Skill Objectives

1. Given three illustrations of wall treatments using brick, ceramic tile, and mirrors, analyze the functional and esthetic characteristics of each.

2. Using two different wall treatments in each room and applying selection criteria for compatible colors, textures, and patterns, develop wall-treatment plans for both an informal and a formal master bedroom.

3. Evaluate new materials that can be used as insulators against noise and heat loss.

ASSIGNMENTS

Before Viewing the Program

□ Review pages 191–207 and read pages 209–215 in the text, noting particularly those terms listed in the glossary in this lesson.

□ Read the comprehension and skill objectives for this lesson in the study guide.

□ Carefully study the overview, highlighting the important points and new concepts.

□ Look over the study activities and study questions for this lesson.

View the Program "Wall to Wall"

While viewing the program, note specifically:

□ samples of various products which can be used for wall treatments.

□ designer Russell Phinder discussing guidelines for combining and coordinating fabrics, paint, and wallpaper in a design plan.

□ how to carry out a design theme using related textiles and textures.

□ examples of wallpaper and fabric groupings which are too dynamic for balance and compatibility.

After Viewing the Program

□ Review the glossary terms and learning objectives.

□ Complete the study activities.

□ Test your understanding of this lesson by answering the study questions at the end of the lesson. Check your answers with the key.

GLOSSARY

(Page numbers refer to your text.)

architectural glass, page 197

ceramic tile, page 197

coffered ceiling, page 209

coordinating wall treatments: wall coverings that have been carefully selected to carry through the mood or color scheme of a room in a manner which is attractive and functional.

coved ceiling, page 210

double glazed, page 343

dropped ceiling, page 212

flat-beamed ceiling, page 210

frescoed ceiling, page 209

gabled ceiling, page 210

masonry: wall coverings or architectural features constructed of brick, stone, tile, or a similar material.

sculptured ceiling, page 212

shed ceiling, page 210

STUDY ACTIVITIES

Required Activities

1. Design a wall treatment plan for the living room of a small condominium. Use a mirror to cover the wall. Then select and describe an interesting, attractive treatment for other walls in the same room.
2. Design a treatment plan for the ceiling of the same room. Assume that the present ceiling is a standard eight-foot, wallboard ceiling, and choose materials that would improve the character or atmosphere of the room.

Extra-Credit Activities

1. Write a two-page paper describing at least one advantage and one disadvantage of each of the following wall-treatment materials: brick, stone, ceramic tile, mirror, and carpeting.
2. Write a one-to-two-page paper explaining how to determine the formality or informality of a wall-treatment product.

STUDY QUESTIONS

(Select the one best answer.)

Comprehension Objective 1:   Identify at least three factors that should be considered when selecting a wall treatment for a room.

1. Which of the following considerations is *least* important when selecting a wall treatment?
   a. room function
   b. color scheme
   c. mood or theme
   d. ease of installation
   e. degree of formality or informality

2. In which of the following locations would mirrors be the best choice as a wall treatment?
   a. a child's nursery or playroom
   b. the dressing area in a small bathroom
   c. framing a used brick fireplace in a small family room
   d. behind or over the sink in a windowless kitchen
   e. all of the above

3. If reducing the noise level in a family room is one of your priorities, which of these wall treatments should be avoided?
   a. solid wood paneling
   b. fabric-covered walls
   c. brick
   d. cork tiles

4. The factor(s) contributing to the growing popularity of using carpeting as a wall covering is (are)
   a. the development of newer, lighter-weight, and more flexible carpeting materials.
   b. the acoustical benefits of muffling sound.
   c. the development of new adhesives that make installation easier.
   d. that carpeting spot cleans well.
   e. stated in all of the above answers.

Comprehension Objective 2:   Identify techniques for planning wall treatments for one room in relation to treatments used in other rooms that may be viewed simultaneously.

5. The easiest, yet most effective way to relate the wall treatments used in a living room and adjacent dining room is to effectively coordinate the
   a. textures.
   b. colors.
   c. patterns.
   d. window coverings.

6. What type of wall treatments have reflective surfaces, very fine textures, light values and lower intensity colors?
   a. formal
   b. informal

7. Which of these materials would be incongruous in an informal setting?
   a. cork wall tiles
   b. dark wood paneling
   c. red clay bricks
   d. mirror panels
   e. grass cloth-covered wall panels

Comprehension Objective 3:   Identify two types of ceiling materials and describe the contribution each makes to a room design plan.

8. _____ for ceilings offer the greatest variety of materials and patterns.
   a. Tiles
   b. Fabrics
   c. Flat wood strips
   d. Glass or plastic panels

9. Which of the following is (are) (a) major advantage(s) of incorporating glass panels into a ceiling design?
   a. It improves additional overhead daylight.
   b. New methods of glazing have improved insulation properties of glass panels.
   c. Recessed artificial lights can be more easily incorporated for better nighttime lighting.
   d. All of the above are advantages.
   e. The advantages are described only in statements a and b.

ANSWER KEY

(Page numbers refer to your text.)

1. d (study guide, television program)
2. b (page 195, study guide)
3. c (page 197)
4. e (page 205, television program)
5. d (study guide)
6. a (page 214)
7. d (pages 214–215)
8. a (page 214)
9. d (pages 214–215)

CASING THE JOINT

OVERVIEW

Although the term **case goods** usually applies to furniture pieces that provide some type of storage, such as buffets, chests of drawers, and consoles, some references identify all furniture that is not upholstered as case goods. In this lesson the term will be used to refer to tables and nonupholstered or partially upholstered chairs, as well as storage pieces.

Wood has been and still remains the most popular material for the construction of case goods. Although well-designed quality pieces can also be made of materials such as plastic, metal, cardboard, glass, and parts of plants (such as rattan, or wicker), this lesson emphasizes the standard characteristics of quality wooden case goods. Many of the criteria for selecting wooden goods can be applied when you select nonwooden pieces, and the television program for this lesson offers many examples.

The most effective way to evaluate the overall quality of case goods is to evaluate the following components: structural and applied design, finish, hardware, and construction materials and techniques. The basic structural design and, if used, applied design, should be evaluated with reference to the principles of design.

Quality case goods with simple lines and little or no applied design are usually less expensive than comparable pieces with additional decorative details. If you prefer pieces with decorative detail, plan to spend more money and carefully evaluate the quality of the design itself, as well as the furniture. Be cautions of wood furniture with excessive "carved effects" created by fixing pieces of simulated wood onto the basic structure. Although it is possible to construct a well-designed quality piece at a reasonable price with this technique, the ostentatious use of simulated products can ruin a basically good design. Sometimes these decorative touches are applied to hide inferior materials and construction techniques.

A beautiful finish on case goods is indicative of quality. Finishes are applied to wood furniture to (1) enhance the natural qualities of the wood, (2) change its color, (3) protect it from damage by heat, moisture, and alcohol, and (4) add decorative effects such as **distressing** and **antiquing**. (To "distress" a piece, manufacturers purposely dent, burn, slash, or scratch the surface to achieve an informal or rustic look.) The type of finish selected should be in accordance with functional and esthetic needs. For example, distressed pieces are excellent for high-use areas because a few additional dents and scratches will usually blend quite well with the original finish. High-quality finishes have a mellow glow, or **patina**, developed by hand rubbing and polishing, and are free of irregularities such as bubbles, brush marks, or extensive buildup of the finish in the crevices.

The design of the **hardware** should be in keeping with the overall design characteristics of the piece. Naturally, quality decorative hardware adds more to the retail price than simply designed structural hardware. Well-made metal hardware is usually heavy and is attached securely through a panel with screws or bolts. Less noticeable hardware pieces, such as hinges, should also be checked for quality and ease in functioning.

To evaluate specific construction details, look for a label indicating the types of materials used. If the information is not easily located, ask the dealer for the catalog that gives an accurate description of the piece.

The term **solid wood** indicates that all exposed parts are constructed with whatever solid wood the manufacturer claims to have used, such as genuine solid walnut. **Hardwoods** such as mahogany and pecan resist dents and scratches and holds joints more securely than such **softer woods** as pine and fir. Many of the beautiful solid hardwoods are premium material and are therefore considerably more expensive than the softer woods. However, special detailed hand carving and other effects can only be accomplished with solid hardwoods. If materials have been used to simulate wood carving, federal law requires that they be identified as such.

Simulated wood includes several types of products. It could be a print of the desired wood imposed on another less expensive wood, or it could be a wood design printed on paper with the addition of a plastic surface coating and a plywood backing. Simulated wood carvings can be constructed of such products as rigid plastics and materials similar to particle board.

Cardboard furniture, including pieces made of laminated fiberply, are reasonably priced and usually quite strong. Because of the construction technique—layers of corrugated cardboard laminated in alternate directions—these pieces are sturdy and can be unusually shaped. Also, cardboard absorbs sound and can have a suedelike surface. These qualities certainly make cardboard furniture an interesting alternative to wood and worthy of some consideration.

Particle board is made by combining wood flakes with a resin binding agent and pressing the mixture into sheets. Because it is less expensive than wood, particle board can be used for unexposed parts of furniture. This construction will help keep the retail prices lower than if the same piece were constructed totally of wood. The exposed surfaces of the particle board may or may not have a hardwood veneer laminated to them.

One of the best ways to determine the quality of construction throughout a piece is to study one of the drawers. The drawer should glide smoothly and have a stop to prevent its being unintentionally pulled all the way out. Although drawer interiors are generally not stained to match the exterior, they should be well sanded and finished. The sides and backs should be made of wood rather than particle board, and the upper edges of the drawer should be rounded. In fine quality case goods, sections are connected by either **dovetail** or **tongue-and-groove** joints. Other strong joining methods used in case goods include the **mortise and tenon**, the **dado**, and the **double dowel**. Although some of these joints are not easily distinguished from the less desirable **butt joint**, a reputable dealer should be able to provide information about the specific construction method used.

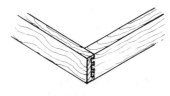

FIGURE 20.1 Dovetail

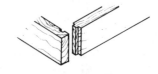

FIGURE 20.2 Tongue and groove

FIGURE 20.3 Mortise and tenon

FIGURE 20.4 Dado joint

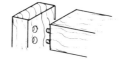

FIGURE 20.5 Double doweling

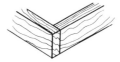

FIGURE 20.6 Butt

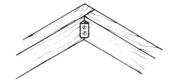

FIGURE 20.7 Reinforced butt

In addition to basic drawer construction, evaluate all other parts for quality materials and workmanship. The better-quality pieces have dust partitions made of plywood or fiberboard between drawers. The lower edges of all tables, chairs, and desks should be smoothly sanded and finished. Some type of corner block should be included for additional stability inside standard joinings of corner sections. By all means, check the overall stability of case goods by applying pressure on all the sides. Beware of a "wobbly" piece.

Additional quality criteria may apply, depending on the specific case goods. For example, when buying an expandable table check the finish and apron details of the table leaves to make sure they match the basic piece. Also, watch for signs of inferior quality in both materials and construction, such as the presence of staples, excessive use of particle board, or poorly matched joinings filled in with glue or other material.

If you apply the suggestions found in this lesson, you will have an excellent foundation for judging the quality of case goods. Additionally, be sure to purchase your case goods from reputable dealers who take pride in their products and in their service to customers.

LEARNING OBJECTIVES

After reading the assignment, viewing the program, and completing the assigned activities, you will be able to accomplish the following objectives:

Comprehension Objectives

1. Define and explain the use of each of the following materials found in case goods construction: hardware, solid wood, veneer, and particle board.
2. Identify the advantages and disadvantages of the following materials used in case goods construction: pine, metal, molded plastic, clear glass.

Skill Objectives

1. Analyze the information on a case-goods label in relation to the use, probable price range, and quality of the piece.
2. Identify and evaluate specific parts of any wood drawer in relation to quality construction.

ASSIGNMENTS

Before Viewing the Program

- ☐ Read pages 243–251 and "Care of Fine Furniture," pages 261–264, in the text, noting particularly those terms listed in the glossary in this lesson.
- ☐ Read the comprehension and skill objectives for this lesson in the study guide.
- ☐ Carefully study the overview, highlighting the important points and new concepts.
- ☐ Look over the study activities and study questions for this lesson.

View the Program "Casing the Joint"

While viewing the program, note specifically:

- ☐ the sequence in the furniture factory showing hand- and machine-carving and other aspects of furniture construction.
- ☐ interior designer Betty Holtz demonstrating the four components of fine quality in case goods.
- ☐ interior construction details and how they are indicators of high-quality construction.
- ☐ other materials that are used to construct nonupholstered furniture and how nonwood pieces can be evaluated to determine quality.

After Viewing the Program

- ☐ Review the glossary terms and learning objectives.
- ☐ Complete the study activities.
- ☐ Test your understanding of this lesson by answering the study questions at the end of the lesson. Check your answers with the key.

GLOSSARY

(Page numbers refer to your text.)

antiquing: finishing a relatively new furniture piece in such a way as to resemble an older style or period.

butt joint, study guide overview

cardboard furniture, study guide overview, television program

case goods, study guide overview, television program

collection, page 246

dado, study guide overview

distressing, study guide overview

double dowel, study guide overview

dovetail, study guide overview

furniture group, page 246

furniture suite, page 246

genuine wood, page 247

hardware, study guide overview, television program

hardwood, page 247

malacca: rattan furniture made with the bark still attached for added durability; can be used outdoors.

miter, page 247, study guide overview

mortise and tenon, page 247, study guide overview

particle board, study guide overview

patina: mellow, rich glow in the finish of wooden furniture

quality-construction characteristics, page 247

simulated wood, study guide overview

softwood, page 247, study guide overview

solid wood, page 247, study guide overview

tongue and groove, page 247, study guide overview

veneer, page 247

STUDY ACTIVITIES

Required Activities

1. Visit a furniture store and examine three case goods items. Apply the four criteria for determining quality discussed in the television program for this lesson and evaluate each item. Write a two-to-three-page paper describing each case goods item and how it does or does not meet the four criteria.
2. Assess one case goods item in your home according to the four criteria. Write a one-to-two-page paper describing the item and your assessment.

Extra-Credit Activities

Choose two of the following assignments to complete. Write a two-page paper responding to each assignment.

□ Identify four characteristics indicative of quality construction in furniture drawers.

□ List one positive esthetic or functional characteristic for each of the following materials used in furniture construction: chrome, fiberply, clear glass, hardwood veneer.

□ Define "veneer" and explain the value of using veneer in furniture construction to the consumer.

□ Describe how to best evaluate the quality of a finish used on case goods.

STUDY QUESTIONS

(Select the one best answer.)

Comprehension Objective 1:   Define and explain the use of each of the following materials found in case goods construction: hardwood, solid wood, veneer, and particle board.

1. The term "solid wood" is an indication that the furniture item
   a. is made entirely from hardwood.
   b. is made either entirely from hardwood or from softwood.
   c. might be made of teak, birch, cherry, oak, maple, or walnut.
   d. could be described by any of the above answers.
   e. could be described by answers a and c.

2. The advantage of using wood veneer for furniture is
   a. increased strength.
   b. reduced warping.
   c. greater variety in surface patterns.
   d. less cost.
   e. described by all of the above.

3. Which of the following is a commonly used softwood?
   a. cherry
   b. pecan
   c. pine
   d. birch
   e. mahogany

4. Which of the following classifications implies the premium grade of wood is being used?
   a. solid wood
   b. genuine wood
   c. wood veneer
   d. particle board

Comprehension Objective 2:   Identify the advantages and disadvantages of the following materials used in case goods construction: pine, metal, molded plastic, clear glass.

5. What is the disadvantage of furniture constructed of pine?
   a. There will be knotty pine holes throughout the piece.
   b. It may be less resistant to dents and scratches than other woods.
   c. Pine is scarce and therefore more costly than other woods.
   d. It will only take one color of wood stain.
   e. It is difficult to carve for decorative effects.

6. Clear glass can add a very attractive dimension when used in case goods construction; however, it
   a. scratches easily.
   b. cannot be used outdoors.
   c. offers no variations in use or construction.
   d. must be kept clean to look good.

7. Which of the following is (are) (a) primary disadvantage(s) of using molded plastic in case goods construction?
   a. A plastic surface scratches easily.
   b. Plastic is cold to sit on and therefore uncomfortable.
   c. Plastic does not take colors well.
   d. Plastic can be damaged by heat.
   e. Both the factors described in a and d apply.

8. The measure of good quality in furnishings constructed of chrome, stainless steel, or brass is
   a. their high cost.
   b. their use of intricate design detail.
   c. a smooth, even finish with no bumps or mars.
   d. described by all of the above.

ANSWER KEY

(Page numbers refer to your text.)

1. e (page 247)
2. e (page 247)
3. c (page 247)
4. a (page 247)
5. b (page 247, television program)
6. d (television program)
7. e (television program)
8. c (television program)

FABRICS ON FRAMES

OVERVIEW

The old saying, "You can't judge a book by its cover," certainly applies when shopping for and selecting upholstered furniture, since many of the checkpoints for quality are concealed by the upholstery itself. However, working knowledge of terminology and construction methods will help you identify quality construction techniques, ask appropriate questions, and select upholstered items that will be durable and attractive.

Quality upholstered furniture is a combination of an exterior of fine fabric with a basic furniture piece of excellent construction and materials. In fact, many interior designers suggest that upholstered furniture should be selected "from the inside out." Well-constructed upholstered furniture will provide many years of durable, comfortable service. While poorly constructed furniture may look good when it is new, within a few weeks or months, it often begins to sag, lump, and become uncomfortable.

Quality construction begins with the **frame**. All frames should be **kiln-dried** and made of quality hardwood such as ash, alder, oak, birch, or maple. The only way you will be able to determine whether a frame has been kiln dried is by the absence of warping or beads of sap. Frame pieces should be joined with a combination of glue and double doweling so that the frame will withstand stress and strain. Corner blocks and screws should be used to reinforce all corners.

To form the base of the seat and back, tightly woven bands of jute or strong **webbing** are interlaced and securely attached to the frame. (An excellent construction is produced by webbing that is closely interlaced and preferably doubled.) Heavy cotton material stretched across the chair bottom, back, or sides, and held tautly in place with tiny springs, is sometimes used instead of webbing. Steel or wooden slats can be used in place of webbing or heavy cotton and springs, but they do not have the necessary elasticity which provides seating comfort.

Highly tempered, enameled steel **coil springs** should be anchored to the webbing or stretched cotton. Twelve springs per seat is the best construction, and eight is the minimum. In better-quality furniture, the springs are tied to each other and to the frame in eight places with heavy hemp or flax twine to keep the springs in place and prevent sagging. Each spring is tied at right angles in two directions and diagonally, resulting in eight knots on each spring. Thus the phrase **"hand tied eight ways"** has come to denote fine-quality construction. Try to determine if the coil springs have been placed close together (not so close as to rub against one another) so that they produce a resilient, comfortable seat called a **"spring-edge seat."** You can check this by touch or ask the retail salesperson.

Other types of springs are used in moderately priced furniture. **Sagless springs** are flat wavy lines of high-quality steel that look like grillwork. They are attached to the top of the frame and produce a **"rigid-edge seat."**

The difference between these two types of spring construction is cost and comfort. The sagless spring is less expensive than the coil spring, but the rigid-edge seat produced is not as comfortable as the soft, spring-edge seat. Although both types of construction can be durable if quality materials and techniques are used, you have to determine if the additional comfort warrants the additional cost.

The next construction step is to cover the springs with burlap. On the front edge of the seat a special reinforcement of rolled burlap is added. This gives the frame a soft edge and keeps the filling layer from working away from the edges.

Next, a layer of **filling** is placed over the burlap. Some fillers used are kapok, sisal, cotton, goose down and feathers, or rubberized hair. **Foam rubber** has also become very popular in medium- to high-priced furniture. Synthetic fibers, sometimes a muslin cover, and finally the upholstery fabric blanket the filler. Even though the muslin cover relieves the extreme stress placed on the upholstery fabric, some manufacturers cut costs by eliminating the muslin.

Guidelines for selecting upholstery fabrics were discussed in a previous lesson. An additional pointer is to make sure that the outer fabric is firm but not too tight. Stretched fabric will eventually lose its stability and sag out of shape. Whatever upholstery fabric is selected, it should be used on all exposed parts and on the seat under any loose cushions. If less-expensive fabric is used on this underseat, it should not be exposed, even when people sit down and the cushions move slightly.

Although any fabric can be used to cover upholstered furniture, a tight weave and a strong yarn will provide the most durability. Be sure to check hang tags for fabric content, finishes, and care. If this information is not available, ask a salesperson.

Even the most concerned consumer will find it almost impossible to personally check the construction quality and type of spring on a finished upholstered piece. For information not listed on the label or determined through inspection, ask the retailer pertinent questions or ask to see a **"spec sheet"** listing the fine points of materials and construction techniques.

Also, consider these additional guidelines for evaluating upholstered furniture prior to purchase:

1. All fabric seams should be straight and inconspicuous.
2. If the upholstery fabric has a pattern, it should be matched at the seams. Loose cushions should form a pattern match with the rest of the sofa or chair.
3. Consider any family allergies before selecting a fabric and filling, as goose down, feathers, and hair can cause allergic reactions. Check the hang tags for fabric and filler content.
4. If extra fabric is desired for matching draperies or bedspreads, be sure to order it at the same time you order the furniture to insure that the dyelots will be the same.
5. Don't overlook the practicality of chair arm protectors tailored from the upholstered fabric.
6. If trims are used, check to see that they are neatly and appropriately applied.

By following the guidelines presented in this lesson, you should be able to buy upholstered furniture that virtually will last a lifetime. But in your search for quality, do not compromise on comfort. Sit on the chair or sofa for an extended time if possible. Notice the angle of the back, the depth and height of the seat, the height of the arms, and the firmness of the cushions. Unless the upholstered piece is comfortable as well as serviceable, you will find yourself hoping it can soon be replaced.

LEARNING OBJECTIVES

After reading the assignment, viewing the program, and completing the assigned activities, you will be able to accomplish the following objectives:

Comprehension Objectives

1. Explain how to evaluate upholstered furniture for comfort and for quality construction.
2. Identify the basic interior components of an upholstered chair having loose seat and back cushions.
3. Identify at least three considerations for determining whether or not to reupholster a used sofa or chair.

Skill Objective

1. Using a sofa upholstered in print fabric, evaluate the exterior according to design principles, quality characteristics, and possible price range.

ASSIGNMENTS

Before Viewing the Program

- Read pages 252–253 in the text, noting particularly those terms listed in the glossary in this lesson.
- Read the comprehension and skill objectives for this lesson in the study guide.
- Carefully study the overview, highlighting the important points and new concepts.
- Look over the study activities and study questions for this lesson.

View the Program "Fabrics on Frames"

While viewing the program, note specifically:

- guidelines for determining the quality of construction in upholstered furniture.
- the importance of the frame in the durability of a chair or sofa.
- factors to consider when deciding on upholstery fabric.
- the pros and cons of using slipcovers rather than reupholstering.
- Dick Stephens, upholstery instructor, discussing how to evaluate an item to determine whether or not it should be reupholstered rather than replaced and the options for restyling during reupholstering.

After Viewing the Program

- Review the glossary terms and learning objectives.
- Complete the study activities.
- Test your understanding of this lesson by answering the study questions at the end of the lesson. Check your answers with the key.

GLOSSARY

(Page numbers refer to your text.)

coil springs, page 252

cotton felt, page 252

double-cone coil spring, page 252

filling, page 252

foam rubber, page 252

frame, page 252

"hand tied eight ways," study guide overview

kiln-dried, study guide overview, television program

polyester filler, page 252

rigid-edge seat, study guide overview

rubberized fibers, page 252

sagless springs, study guide overview

shredded fibers, page 252

single-cone coil spring, page 252

sinuous wire spring, page 252

slip seat, page 253

"spec sheet," study guide overview

spring-edge seat, study guide overview

square cushion, page 253

T-shaped cushion, page 253

urethane, page 252

webbing, page 252

STUDY ACTIVITIES

Required Activities

1. Visit a furniture store. Ask the sales person if you can see a cross section of the upholstery method used in one of the sofas in their showroom. Write a two-page paper evaluating the quality of construction, using the guidelines presented in this lesson.
2. Examine the label of an upholstered item in a furniture store. Ask the salesperson for information not shown on the label. Then ask to see the "spec sheet." List all the information you obtained from each of these three sources.

Extra-Credit Activity

1. Write a one-to-two-page paper identifying three factors that will generally cause an upholstered piece to have a higher retail price.

STUDY QUESTIONS

(Select the one best answer.)

Comprehension Objective 1:   Explain how to evaluate upholstered furniture for comfort and for quality construction.

1. The best indicator of comfort in a sofa is
   a. having the arms the right height.
   b. knowing what type of springs are inside.
   c. having a soft-textured fabric covering.
   d. sitting in the sofa for an extended time.
   e. all of the above.

2. A good quality sofa frame should be
   a. constructed of kiln-dried hardwood.
   b. nailed *and* glued together for extra strength.
   c. made of molded plastic with steel reinforcements.
   d. all of the above.

3. The type of spring which provides maximum comfort in deep seated upholstered goods is
   a. a single-cone coil.
   b. a double-cone coil.
   c. a sinuous wire.
   d. either a single-cone coil or a sinuous wire.

4. Which of the following is *not* a criterion for selecting satisfactory cushioning for a sofa or chair?
   a. shape retention
   b. ease of cleaning
   c. construction materials which are odorless and nonallergenic
   d. fabric availability in contemporary colors
   e. cushions which stay in place with no slipping or shifting

Comprehension Objective 2:   Identify the basic interior components of an upholstered chair having loose seat and back cushions.

5. Loose cushions in a square shape are generally considered more functional than T-shaped cushions.
   a. true
   b. false

6. Which of the following filling materials represents the *poorest* quality?
   a. polyester
   b. rubberized fibers
   c. foam rubber
   d. urethane foam

7. The spring construction which is particularly suitable for slim-line, contemporary furniture is
   a. single-cone coil.
   b. double-cone coil.
   c. sinuous wire.
   d. woven jute or plastic webbing.

8. Double-cone coils are mounted on a base of
   a. strips of webbing.
   b. strips of metal.
   c. foam.
   d. either strips of webbing or metal.

Comprehension Objective 3: Identify at least three considerations for determining whether or not to reupholster a used sofa or chair.

9. When deciding to reupholster a piece of furniture, it should be evaluated for having
   a. a style which is basically satisfactory.
   b. a hardwood frame that does not twist.
   c. double dowel joints and coil springs.
   d. all of the above features.
   e. the features described in b and c.

10. Slipcovers are an inexpensive way to avoid having to reupholster a piece of furniture.
    a. true
    b. false

ANSWER KEY

(Page numbers refer to your text.)

1. d (page 253, television program)
2. a (study guide)
3. b (page 252)
4. d (page 252, television program)
5. a (page 253)

6. b (page 252)
7. c (page 252)
8. d (page 252)
9. d (television program)
10. b (television program)

FURNITURE
MIX AND MATCH

OVERVIEW

In the past, fashion dictated that rooms be planned around one distinct furniture style, such as American Colonial. Naturally this approach represented a very easy method for achieving a harmonious look among furniture pieces. Today, however, most people have acquired an appreciation for the more unique, interesting effects created by an eclectic plan, one that incorporates a mixture of several furniture styles in a complementary scheme. Mixing and matching furniture styles to enhance the mood or theme in a room has created a vibrant new look in interior design.

Eclectic designing provides not only an interesting and attractive design effect but also the possibility of using your existing furniture pieces with those of differing styles that you add in the future. Also, you can collect several special pieces over a period of years and see them blend well into an established scheme. A primary advantage of learning to mix a variety of furniture styles successfully is that the rooms will be highly individual and personalized.

The text assignment and the television program for this lesson provide a number of guidelines and helpful ideas for successfully coordinating furniture styles. However, the combining of furniture is particularly subject to personal preferences. You may prefer creating a structured, organized environment by "matching" rather than "mixing" the various design components instead of adding the additional spark of a totally out-of-character piece in an otherwise unified setting.

Whether your design plan is eclectic or unified, you will find it helpful to know the general categories of furniture styles. While it is not essential to learn all the design characteristics of specific styles, you will be able to better understand and discuss furniture if you are aware of the basic characteristics of **traditional**, **provincial**, **contemporary**, and **modern styles**. This knowledge will help you communicate your furniture needs and preferences to sales personnel.

The furniture identification charts on pages 262–263 of your text illustrate basic furniture items and styles. Although the illustrations depict specific styles, the terminology can be appropriately applied to similar pieces of a different style. For example, the side chair illustrated on page 263 could be made with straight, classical Louis XVI lines or the ornate qualities characteristic of the **Victorian** style. Further, libraries, manufacturers' catalogs, and retail stores are excellent resources for obtaining information related to furniture styles.

The following guidelines will also help you create a cohesive design plan, whether you are taking the eclectic or the more uniform approach to combining furniture pieces.

- Determine the degree of formality desired in the room. Evaluate each of the pieces of furniture you have, or will be adding, according to this mood.
- Select furnishing components for the room—such as colors, textures, and patterns for the background areas, furniture, and accessories—that express a similar degree of formality.
- Consider refinishing or reupholstering some of your present furniture pieces to make them more compatible with the mood you are attempting to achieve.
- Use large, dominant, or highly decorative pieces as focal points. Employ less emphatic pieces and subordinate background areas in close relationship to the focal points.
- Use transitional pieces that express the same degree of formality to help pull together a variety of distinct styles.
- Consider using a **tripod** or a grouping of three various items, such as three different wood colors or upholstery fabrics. These pieces provide unity through a complementary relationship with one another; they also provide variety within the room.
- Rather than studying all of the various furniture styles simultaneously, you might find it easier to study the styles of one particular country in the sequence of their development.

The television program presents only one interior designer's opinions on how to develop attractive eclectic rooms; however, Ms. Holtz's guidelines provide an excellent foundation upon which to add your own and others' ideas. While the room settings shown on the program express a certain degree of formality, the same criteria can be applied to developing an eclectic blend for the most rustic setting imaginable.

Ms. Holtz emphasizes the importance of compatibility among all components within a room. For example, the colors, patterns, and textures selected for fabrics, background surfaces, and accessories play a vital role in achieving a successful blend. But that is not all. Sometimes these components may be compatible, but the actual combination of furniture pieces is incongruent, and a successful blend is not achieved. Creating a well-designed eclectic room is highly dependent on the ability to select and coordinate *all* of the components within the room so that the total composition expresses unity.

LEARNING OBJECTIVES

After reading the assignment, viewing the program, and completing the assigned activities, you will be able to accomplish the following objectives:

Comprehension Objectives

1. Define the following terms as they relate to furniture selection: suite, furniture group, and collection.
2. Describe the specific characteristics of the general categories of furniture styles: informal, provincial, formal traditional, contemporary, and modern.
3. Explain the influence of the Victorian era, the country look, American Southwest, and Oriental design in today's interiors.

Skill Objectives

1. Examine and compare the differences between an antique, a reproduction, and an adaptation.
2. Select an illustration of eclectic interior design and analyze whether or not the furniture pieces represent good coordination.

ASSIGNMENTS

Before Viewing the Program

□ Review pages 243–253 and read pages 253–264 in the text, noting particularly those terms listed in the glossary in this lesson.
□ Read the comprehension and skill objectives for this lesson in the study guide.
□ Carefully study the overview, highlighting the important points and new concepts.
□ Look over the study activities and study questions for this lesson.

View the Program "Furniture Mix and Match"

While viewing the program, note specifically:

□ Ms. Yablonski's definitions of the terms traditional, provincial, contemporary, modern, and eclectic.
□ typical characteristics of various furniture styles.
□ Betty Holtz, interior designer, discussing the components of two sample rooms and presenting guidelines for developing a compatible mixture of furniture styles.
□ the "tripod concept" as applied to color, wood, fabric, accessories, and furniture.
□ how to select items that enhance either a formal or an informal mood in a room.
□ suggestions for other sources and experiences for learning more about furniture mix and match.

After Viewing the Program

□ Review the glossary terms and learning objectives.
□ Complete the study activities.
□ Test your understanding of this lesson by answering the study questions at the end of the lesson. Check your answers with the key.

GLOSSARY

(Page numbers refer to your text.)
adaptation, page 254
antique, page 254
armoire, page 254
breakfront, page 256

STUDY ACTIVITIES

Required Activities

1. Visit several furniture showrooms and examine merchandise ranging in price from high to low. Compare the quality of design, craftsmanship, and materials used. Write a three-page paper describing your conclusions about (1) spending your interior design dollars and (2) your own personal taste in furnishings.
2. Select a furniture style you like and gather at least five illustrations of the most attractive, versatile pieces representing that style.

Extra-Credit Activity

Write a two-page paper describing five guidelines that are helpful in achieving a well-designed, eclectic room setting.

STUDY QUESTIONS

(Select the one best answer.)

Comprehension Objective 1: Define the following terms as they relate to furniture selection: suite, furniture group, and collection.

1. A collection of furniture is best defined as
   a. a grouping of furniture of the same design.
   b. all furniture intended for use in the same room.
   c. the newest line shown each year at furniture trade shows.
   d. a mixture of pieces acquired over a period of time, all with a feeling of compatibility.

2. Furniture of the same design that has pieces for the bedroom, dining room, and living room is known as a
   a. furniture suite.
   b. furniture group.
   c. furniture collection.
   d. show line.

3. The advantage(s) of buying pieces from a particular group is (are)
   a. that cost is usually lower.
   b. that matching pieces can be added at a later date.
   c. that wood tones and fabrics will not clash.
   d. stated in all of the above answers.

Comprehension Objective 2:   Describe the specific characteristics of the general categories of furniture styles: informal provincial, formal traditional, contemporary, and modern.

4. A furnishing style characterized by a feeling of unpretentious homeyness and of being "lived-in" is known as
   a. Early American.
   b. transitional.
   c. informal provincial.
   d. either Early American or informal provincial.

5. The key word in modern design is
   a. functionalism.
   b. contemporary.
   c. coordinated.
   d. art deco.
   e. transition.

6. Which of the following characteristics is *not* typical of formal traditional styling?
   a. damask, velvet, and brocade fabrics
   b. Aubusson or oriental rugs
   c. pine paneling and plank floors
   d. soft, pastel colors
   e. smooth textures, highly polished woods

7. Contemporary and modern furnishings are primarily designed with emphasis on
   a. comfort.
   b. convenience.
   c. durability.
   d. all of the above factors.
   e. only the factors described in a and c.

Comprehension Objective 3:   Explain the influence of the Victorian era, the country look, American Southwest, and Oriental design in today's interiors.

8. The furnishing style which includes the use of natural materials, simple styling, and a lack of ornamentation is known as
   a. the country look.
   b. Oriental design.
   c. American Southwest design.
   d. the Victorian influence.

9. Marble-topped tables, excessively carved love seats upholstered in red velvet, and the use of small statuary are all typical of
   a. informal provincial styling.
   b. the Victorian era.
   c. formal traditional styling.
   d. the Queen Anne period.
   e. the Roman influence.

10. Geometric patterns in hand-woven rugs, brightly colored wool embroidery, folk images, and shiny tinware are all accessories typical of
    a. American Southwest styling.
    b. the French country look.
    c. the English country look.
    d. Oriental design.

ANSWER KEY

(Page numbers refer to your text.)

1. d (page 246)
2. b (page 246)
3. b (page 246)
4. d (page 254)
5. a (page 257)

6. c (page 255)
7. d (page 257)
8. b (page 258)
9. b (page 259)
10. a (page 259)

NOOKS AND CRANNIES

OVERVIEW

Each room in a home has a predominate and traditional function. However, depending on how available space is planned and organized, any room can serve other specialized and unique needs. For example, a family room that has been traditionally planned for television viewing, reading, and conversation can be customized to include storage and facilities for viewing family movies, a home/office study center, or even artistic pursuits. Bedrooms provide areas for sleeping, dressing, and possibly for reading or study, but they also can be planned to meet special hobby needs such as model building and collecting.

Well-planned **special-purpose areas** and **rooms** obviously increase the usefulness of a home, but they can also enhance esthetic qualities and psychological satisfaction. Providing space and adequate storage for all activities decreases clutter and relieves the frustrations that develop when people live in poorly planned environments. Special-purpose areas and rooms encourage family members to participate in activities that they might otherwise ignore. Also, well-designed, built-in work and storage units can improve the appearance of less-than-perfect room features, such as awkwardly located fireplaces or windows.

Usually, because of limited space, special-purpose areas are incorporated into a room that also serves other needs. However, when space is available, and your life style dictates, you may decide to devote an entire room to a specialized activity. A sewing room and a photographer's darkroom are good examples.

Planning for special-purpose areas or rooms should take place as you develop all the other aspects of a room's design. Make one-fourth-inch scale two-dimensional drawings of the area you wish to customize and include elevations of freestanding and built-in furniture as well as the interior spaces of the storage units. The drawings will help you determine if your special needs will be satisfied and how these spaces, when furnished, will relate to the other design components within the same room.

One decision that needs to be made when planning specialized spaces is whether or not to use individual furniture pieces or custom built-in units. Here are some questions to consider when making your decision:

□ Do you have a mobile life style? If so, you may need **modular**, freestanding, or wall-mounted units that are easily moved and adaptable to new environments.

□ Are ready-made pieces available that satisfy your requirements? Be sure to check for appropriate size, quality, special finishes, and custom details.
□ What is the cost difference between ready-made pieces and custom-built units?
□ Would individual pieces or one custom unit create the most pleasing effect? You might evaluate the possibility of using specially built modular pieces that, when used together, give the illusion of one custom-built unit.
□ Would the location and type of built-in unit enhance or detract from the resale value of the home?

Because special-purpose areas almost always require storage—provided by separate furniture pieces, **customized storage** built-ins, or a combination of these—this program concentrates on efficient storage planning to satisfy a variety of needs. As you view the program, try to determine how you could incorporate some of the ideas and suggestions to improve existing specialized areas or develop new ones in your home.

If you do decide to use the services of a cabinetmaker, either to build new units or to customize existing furniture pieces or cabinets, remember the importance of good communication and be sure to clearly assign responsibilities at the onset of the project. Each person involved should agree upon exactly what the design entails, what materials are to be used, how much the job will cost, how long it will take, how the work is to be financed, and what the quality of the finished product should be.

A variety of services may or may not be provided by the builder, such as developing plan drawings for approval, purchasing all the materials, and completing the finished details of the piece. If you want to decrease the overall cost of the job you might like to finish some of the work yourself or buy the materials at sale prices.

LEARNING OBJECTIVES

After reading the assignment, viewing the program, and completing the assigned activities, you will be able to accomplish the following objectives:

Comprehension Objectives

1. Cite examples of special-purpose areas or rooms and explain the key elements in their design.
2. Describe the steps in planning a special-purpose area or room that satisfies functional and esthetic needs.

Skill Objectives

1. Given a list of needs and available space, complete an appropriate elevation and interior scale drawing for built-in storage.
2. Determine the functional needs for an existing closet, cupboard, or drawer and describe a plan for customizing this area to satisfy needs.

ASSIGNMENTS

Before Viewing the Program

□ Read pages 284–285 in the text.

- Read the comprehension and skill objectives and the glossary items for this lesson in the study guide.
- Carefully study the overview, highlighting the important points and new concepts.
- Look over the study activities and study questions for this lesson.

View the Program "Nooks and Crannies"

While viewing the program, note specifically:

- Jean Taylor, kitchen design specialist, describing the four primary needs of a special-purpose area or room.
- Ms. Taylor's needs and preferences assessment for her client's kitchen.
- how kitchen design concepts apply to other special-purpose areas, such as Ms. Yablonski's home office area and sewing room.
- efficiency in storage and function as exemplified by the movable sewing cabinet.

After Viewing the Program

- Review the glossary terms and learning objectives.
- Complete the study activities.
- Test your understanding of this lesson by answering the study questions at the end of the lesson. Check your answers with the key.

GLOSSARY

customized storage: individually designed and built storage units which meet specific needs for the area they serve.

modular units: standardized units of storage that can be interchanged and moved about for greater flexibility.

special-purpose area or room: a specific room or area in a home where specialized activities are performed, such as a sewing area, photography darkroom, laundry room, or home office.

STUDY ACTIVITIES

Required Activities

1. Choose an existing closet, cupboard, or drawer and list storage needs which could be satisfied by redesigning this area. Develop a two-dimensional, one-fourth-inch scale elevation drawing of the interior of this space as customized to meet the established needs.
2. Identify one special-purpose need you have for your home. Write a one-to-two-page paper discussing how planning to satisfy this need could improve the functional, esthetic, and psychological qualities of your living environment and describing a plan to meet these needs.

Extra-Credit Activity

List three factors to consider when determining whether to use individual furniture pieces or a custom-built unit to satisfy special-purpose needs.

STUDY QUESTIONS

(Select the one best answer.)

Comprehension Objective 1:   Cite examples of special-purpose areas or rooms and explain the key elements in their design.

1. An example of a special-purpose room is a
   a. kitchen.
   b. family room.
   c. sewing room.
   d. bedroom.

2. The key word to designing a satisfying special-purpose room or area is
   a. function.
   b. beauty.
   c. cost.
   d. priorities.

3. Which of the following elements is *not* presented in the television program as essential to a well-planned special-purpose area?
   a. workspace
   b. closet space
   c. lighting
   d. seating
   e. storage

Comprehension Objective 2:   Describe the steps in planning a special-purpose area or room that satisfies functional and esthetic needs.

4. The first step in developing a design plan for a special-purpose room is to
   a. obtain an estimate from a cabinetmaker.
   b. shop for modular pieces to use.
   c. decide on a color scheme.
   d. evaluate the needs of those using the area.

5. Which of the following is (are) often overlooked during special-purpose design because of the focus on correcting the faults of a room or area?
   a. the amount of time spent in the room or area
   b. maintaining the desirable features
   c. whether some work can be done by the owner or occupant of the home
   d. all of the above factors

6. Drawings of storage units need not be done to scale since the cabinetmaker knows what space is required.
   a. true
   b. false

7. Special-purpose areas or rooms are the only exception to the idea that a well-designed room has unity, balance, good proportion, and a center of interest.
   a. true
   b. false

ANSWER KEY

1. c (study guide, television program)
2. a (television program)
3. b (television program)
4. d (television program)
5. a (television program)
6. b (television program)
7. b (television program)

LESSON
24

A ROOM CHECK

OVERVIEW

Thus far in this course you have learned how to develop specific plans for furniture arrangement, use of space, storage, lighting, and fabric coordination. This lesson will help you to understand how to apply what you have learned from preceding lessons and how to integrate these smaller plans into a functional, **complete plan**.

A complete plan not only includes the selection and placement of all design details, but also incorporates structural components such as plumbing, electrical facilities, and built-ins. In addition to satisfying your basic functional and esthetic requirements, you should also include the special considerations unique to each family: factors such as budget limitations, maintenance requirements, and accommodations for physical limitations.

When you coordinate a complete plan, you probably will find it almost impossible to weigh all requirements against the same standard. For example, "givens" in an interior, such as structural materials, color of carpeting and flooring, or presently owned furnishings must be taken into consideration when planning, even if these existing features are not exactly your preference. Also, having a room function at its peak efficiency (i.e., having it serve a variety of practical purposes) may mean having to settle for less-than-ideal esthetic choices. However, by knowing how to use design elements effectively, you can often create illusions of camouflage or correct these choices.

Complete planning gives you the opportunity to identify your priorities, recognize and correct problems, and determine when trade-offs are necessary before you begin purchasing. A comprehensive plan is needed for every room. Rooms such as kitchens and bathrooms, which have well-defined functions and established fixtures and storage, may require less time to plan than other spaces. But even in these very functional rooms the benefits to be derived from careful planning are significant.

Your text provides excellent information to consider when developing plans for specific rooms. Since it would be impossible to include every unique problem, pay particular attention to the basic factors to consider when designing a variety of rooms.

As you view the television program for this lesson, notice the processes involved in developing complete plans for the situations shown. In each case, the individuals identify their specific functional needs as well as their desired esthetic qualities for the rooms. Ideally, complete plans should have been developed for the **multipurpose** living **room** and kitchen-family room before any design changes were implemented. However, designing under less-than-ideal circumstances is a common occurrence, and it is beneficial to develop a complete plan even if you have already begun making some design changes.

In each television case study, the functional needs receive priority in the designing phase and are followed by selecting various coordinated samples that satisfy personal preferences. As you view the plans and **architectural renderings**, you may realize that you have different requirements for the same rooms or prefer another mood, color scheme, or furniture style. The plans shown were developed to meet the needs of specific individuals and represent only one of several ways to design each room.

Since professionally prepared **architectural renderings** (perspective drawings that depict the architect's conception of a finished room) are expensive, they are seldom part of a complete plan. They are presented in this program to help you visualize the rooms as they will appear when completely furnished. With concentrated effort and continued practice, you can learn to visualize a completed room without these drawings.

A truly complete plan does not focus exclusively on the interior of the home, and it is important to consider how the exterior facade and outdoor spaces are related to the interior. Usually when the interior of a home is designed, many possibilities exist for improving the total living environment through thoughtful planning of **extended spaces**. Such areas as garages, carports, balconies, patios, and outdoor spaces may seem to have little relationship to the design of the home's interior, but when these spaces are planned in relation to the inside areas, they can solve problems in the interior.

For example, garages and carports can provide additional storage, create space for certain hobbies, and yield areas for cleanup. Outdoor areas can also create a visual extension of the interior and increase total living space by providing areas for outside dining, recreation, and entertainment.

To maximize extended spaces, apply the same basic guidelines and planning steps as in the development of interior room plans. Careful attention should be given to such factors as ease of maintenance, electrical outlets, lighting, storage, and plumbing. Finally, extended spaces should relate esthetically to the interior of the home.

When you have studied the functions of the various rooms in your home, decide on color preferences, established budget limits, scrutinized your existing furnishings, and considered how the interior plan relates to the exterior, then you are ready to create your complete design plan. However, remember that during the implementation of any plan, the key to satisfaction and success is flexibility.

LEARNING OBJECTIVES

After reading the assignment, viewing the program, and completing the assigned activities, you will be able to accomplish the following objectives:

Comprehension Objectives

1. Describe how several specific design plans can be coordinated into one complete interior design plan.
2. Explain how visual and living space within a dwelling can be increased by well-designed outdoor living areas.

Skill Objectives

1. Given a specific hobby or function, describe two possible room designs to accommodate the activities. Include such functions as space, lighting, furniture, plumbing, storage, and electrical outlets.
2. Design a room to be used for at least three different activities, satisfying space, storage, furniture, and maintenance requirements.

ASSIGNMENTS

Before Viewing the Program

☐ Read pages 291–317 in the text.
☐ Read the comprehension and skill objectives for this lesson in the study guide.
☐ Carefully study the overview, highlighting the important points and new concepts.
☐ Look over the study activities and study questions for this lesson.

View the Program "A Room Check"

While viewing the program, note specifically:

☐ guidelines for integrating specific design plans into one complete plan.
☐ how complete plans were developed for a multipurpose living room, a combination kitchen-family room, and a kitchen with an eating area.
☐ the use of exterior areas such as garage or back yard to extend the function of interior areas.
☐ Fred Lang, landscape architect, explaining how to maximize outdoor space and provide visual and functional integration between interior and exterior designs.

After Viewing the Program

☐ Review the glossary terms and learning objectives.
☐ Complete the study activities.
☐ Test your understanding of this lesson by answering the study questions at the end of the lesson. Check your answers with the key.

GLOSSARY

architectural renderings: perspective drawings that depict the architect's conception of a finished room.

complete plan: a total functional plan for specific use of space, storage, lighting, furniture selection and coordination, color and fabric selection, and the structural components of a home.

extended spaces: areas adjacent to but outside the major living areas, such as garages, carports, balconies, patios, pool or hot tub areas.

multipurpose room: any room which provides for more than one function, activity, or purpose.

STUDY ACTIVITIES

Required Activities

1. Create an organized file of at least twenty specific solutions for rooms that have problem multipurpose areas. Write a two-page paper explaining how you could satisfactorily apply five of these solutions in your present environment.
2. Write a two-to-three-page paper analyzing any furnished room as to how successfully it incorporates all components into a complete plan. Suggest changes that would improve the complete plan.

Extra-Credit Activities

1. Write a one-to-two-page paper explaining the differences between a complete plan and an individual plan such as a furniture-arrangement plan, a lighting plan, or a fabric-coordination plan.
2. List and describe at least six factors that should be considered when designing a room to accommodate a particular hobby or function.

STUDY QUESTIONS

(Select the one best answer.)

Comprehension Objective 1:   Describe how several specific design plans can be coordinated into one complete interior design plan.

1. Which of the following is an (are) advantage(s) of working with a complete design plan?
   a. It helps identify priorities.
   b. It allows you to recognize and correct problems.
   c. It helps determine when trade-offs are necessary before making purchases.
   d. All of the above factors are advantages.
   e. The factors described in a and b are advantages.
2. The more functional rooms such as kitchens and bathrooms usually require less time for developing a complete plan.
   a. true
   b. false
3. Plumbing, electrical facilities, and built ins are important considerations in developing a complete design plan.
   a. true
   b. false

Comprehension Objective 2:   Explain how visual living space within a dwelling can be increased by well-designed outdoor living areas.

4. Which of the following is *not* an example of extended space?
   a. a balcony
   b. a garage or carport
   c. a patio
   d. a laundry room
   e. a pool or hot tub area

5. Well-designed outdoor living areas can enhance interior living space by
    a. providing an attractive view.
    b. offering additional entertainment space.
    c. visually enlarging the interior living space.
    d. providing space for outdoor dining.
    e. doing all of the above.
6. Planning extended spaces requires slightly different guidelines or planning steps than those used for developing interior plans.
    a. true
    b. false

ANSWER KEY

1. d (study guide, television program)
2. a (television program)
3. a (study guide)
4. d (study guide, television program)
5. e (study guide, television program)
6. b (study guide, television program)

THE PERSONAL STAMP

OVERVIEW

Accessorizing is the most intimate, personal part of interior design. It is also one of the most important. When the major walls and furnishings lack color and warmth, accessories can easily remedy the situation. A plain or sparsely furnished room begins to come alive when well-chosen accessories are added. Accessories can be used to establish the major color scheme of a room. Finally, accessories can frequently complete the balance, provide emphasis, and establish rhythmic eye movement within a home environment.

A basic guideline for selecting and arranging accessories is to keep in mind the elements and principles of design, as well as the interrelationship of shapes, colors, and textures. Accessory and furniture sizes should be in proportion to one another and to the room as a whole, as well as similar in their degree of formality or informality. Although the compatibility of a piece with its environment is important, accessories should be selected primarily because they please you and your family. Neither the style nor the motif of furniture and accessories must match. Rules are secondary, and a deviation from the usual may be just the spark your home needs. Train your eye to recognize what constitutes a beautiful composition of accessories. One very prominent designer feels that the only way to tell what does or does not go together is to experiment with a variety of pieces.

Nothing adds more warmth and personality to a room than objects you cherish, and accessories should tell visitors about the character of the people living in the home. Personality and interests should be expressed. This not only invites conversation, but brings enjoyment to the occupants when special treasures are on display for others to appreciate and admire.

Accessories can be categorized as **functional** or **decorative**, and some can be described as both. Specific purpose items such as lamps, clocks, mirrors, books, pillows, ashtrays, vases, and tableware are considered functional. But with just a little imagination, such items can be made very appealing. Small functional items may be clustered for attention and appeal. For example, ashtrays and lighters grouped with an antique humidor or pipe collection provide more visual excitement than if they were placed randomly about the room. Objects chosen for their beauty alone are decorative accessories. These can include paintings, pottery, floral arrangements, plants, crafts, personal collections, and family photographs.

Accessory choices are virtually unlimited. Interesting and inexpensive items can be found everywhere and incorporated throughout your home. You may find some exciting ways to

155

brighten your home when you use salvaged "junk" with imagination. Keep your eyes open when viewing model homes, retail displays, friends' homes, or when traveling. Perhaps the most exciting source of accessories is your own inventiveness.

Generally a wall area is a good beginning point for accessorizing, as walls generally provide the most opportunity for dramatic impact. However, do not position wall or any other accessories without a total effect in mind. Although some individuals have the talent to create successful compositions without forethought, most find that a careful plan helps them implement creative ideas and even helps them distract the eye from design problems within the room. When planning wall accessories, keep in mind that opposite walls should have comparable visual weight and the room should appear balanced.

Wall arrangements can be preplanned in several ways. You can use templates of your accessories on a one-fourth-inch scale wall elevation, or you can draw a full-scale plan on brown paper and tape it to the wall for examination. You can also block out the size of the wall area on the floor with pieces of string and experiment with your accessories in this space.

Surface accessories divide and soften the visual expanses found in most rooms. The number used in a room or area depends on personal taste, style of accessories, and the mood of the room. Some people prefer tastefully "organized clutter"; others like "streamlined emptiness." Sometimes the degree of accessorizing is a practical matter. For example, it would be impractical for a family with small children to incorporate numerous surface accessories into the design of the home.

These additional guidelines will help you to achieve satisfying and successful results with accessories:

- Develop a list of needed accessories and compare it with what you already have.
- Plants, paintings, and lamps draw the eyes into corners and make the room seem more spacious.
- Accessories are generally placed where people normally look, where you want people to look, and at eye level.
- Groupings should contain a variety of shapes for a more interesting composition.
- Work from a center hub when you place groupings, thereby keeping the viewer's eye contained.
- Space between items in a grouping should be limited to less than the dimension of the largest item in the grouping. However, the arrangement should not be crowded.
- Achieve three-dimensional variety on walls by using items such as deep frames or plants.
- Notice the relationships of objects to their backgrounds and to one another.
- Wall accessories should be anchored by having a piece of furniture beneath them, one that has greater visual weight than the accessories.

One of the most satisfying and creative aspects of accessories is that they need not be static. Simple rearrangements and variation of placement can produce a refreshing new look in your room. Some people even enjoy rotating their accessories. Seasonal items or accessories that have temporarily lost their appeal, when brought out after a period of storage, can bring vibrant renewal to the design of the home.

LEARNING OBJECTIVES

After reading the assignment, viewing the program, and completing the assigned activities, you will be able to accomplish the following objectives:

Comprehension Objectives

1. Identify at least three reasons for using accessories in an interior and describe basic guidelines for their use.
2. Cite several common sources of accessories and identify the criteria for selecting an item as an accessory.

Skill Objectives

1. Using both functional and decorative accessories, arrange and discuss well-planned accessory groupings for each of two given surface areas.
2. Given a furnished interior, analyze the selection and placement of functional and decorative accessories in relation to the principles of design.

ASSIGNMENTS

Before Viewing the Program

□ Read pages 318–325 in the text, noting particularly those items listed in the glossary in this lesson.
□ Read the comprehension and skill objectives for this lesson in the study guide.
□ Carefully study the overview, highlighting the important points and new concepts.
□ Look over the study activities and study questions for this lesson.

View the Program "The Personal Stamp"

While viewing the program, note specifically:

□ examples of both decorative and functional accessories.
□ the appearance of a room that is well furnished but not accessorized.
□ Designer Carole Eichen's suggestions for the selection, placement, and maintenance of accessories.
□ concepts and guidelines used when planning and creating a picture wall.
□ the importance of "collectibles" in expressing individual experiences and interests.
□ suggestions for selecting, arranging, and grouping table accessories.

After Viewing the Program

□ Review the glossary terms and learning objectives.
□ Complete the study activities.
□ Test your understanding of this lesson by answering the study questions at the end of the lesson. Check your answers with the key.

GLOSSARY

(Page numbers refer to your text.)

Coromandel screen, pages 318, 343

decorative accessories, study guide overview

escutcheon, page 344

functional accessories, study guide overview

surface accessories: decorative or functional accessories that are used as horizontal surfaces, such as shelves, or table tops.

STUDY ACTIVITIES

Required Activities

FIGURE 25.1

1. Using this artist's rendition of the picture wall created in the television program for
this lesson, write a two-to-three-page paper identifying the important accessorizing
guidelines pointed out by the designer, Carole Eichen. What, if any, guidelines did
she overlook? How would you approach the same situation? Which parts of the
arrangement appeal to you? Which do not? Why?

2. Examine the accessories used within your own home. How do these accessories
reflect you or your family's personality and life style? Determine how a regrouping
of a wall arrangement or of a surface composition could bring about a refreshing
change in the room. Write a two-to-three-page paper describing your accessories and
your conclusions about their best arrangements.

Extra-Credit Activities

1. Write a two-page paper comparing and contrasting the room accessorized by Carole
Eichen with the accessorized room as illustrated on page 266 of your text.

2. Books, plants, and fresh or dried flowers blend well with any accessory plan. Visit a friend's home or a model home and determine how the use of these items produces a warm, inviting feeling, or how the items could be added to "humanize" the present design. Write a two-page paper describing your findings.

STUDY QUESTIONS

(Select the one best answer.)

Comprehension Objective 1: Identify at least three reasons for using accessories in an interior and describe basic guidelines for their use.

1. Which of the following functions can careful accessorizing accomplish in a home?
   a. providing emphasis
   b. establishing rhythmic eye movement
   c. completing the balance
   d. making a room "come alive"
   e. all of the above functions

2. When planning and placing accessories, remember
   a. that flat objects should be placed or hung on the wall.
   b. that matched pairs of items are easier to arrange in an informal manner.
   c. to consider the interrelationship of color, size, shape, and texture.
   d. all of the above factors.
   e. the factors described in a and c.

3. It is not important that the style or motif of your accessories match the furnishings, but it is important that the mood of formality or informality be consistent.
   a. true
   b. false

Comprehension Objective 2: Cite several common sources of accessories and identify the criteria for selecting an item as an accessory.

4. The most important reason(s) for selecting an item as an accessory is (are) that it
   a. has historic value.
   b. was a gift.
   c. is meaningful or beautiful to the owner.
   d. is expensive and unique.
   e. meets the criteria described in a and c.

5. Which of the following are *not* considered functional accessories?
   a. fireplace tools
   b. wastebaskets
   c. clocks
   d. flowers
   e. lamps

6. A good source of either decorative or functional accessories is
   a. flea market "treasures."
   b. gifts of sentimental value.
   c. souvenirs of personal travels.
   d. family heirlooms.
   e. any of the above.

7. Functional items such as large decorative screens or small drawer pulls on a chest are not considered to be accessories.
    a. true
    b. false

LESSON
26

PULLING IT ALL TOGETHER

OVERVIEW

This final telecourse lesson expands upon many of the concepts presented in earlier lessons. The importance of **transitional flow** throughout the rooms of a home is emphasized, as well as the importance of considering and evaluating possible interior and exterior **architectural changes** during early design planning phases. This lesson also presents a sequential work plan for actually implementing your design ideas. Additionally, the reading assignment in your text will provide information about the career possibilities in interior design.

In a home characterized by "transitional flow," adjacent rooms have a significant design relationship and the viewer's eyes travel smoothly from one room to another. When transitional flow is successfully executed, the home is esthetically more attractive, the environment is psychologically more relaxing, and (because the total interior space has fewer visual divisions) the size of areas may even appear larger. Before you begin to implement your designs, then, evaluate each of your room plans as it relates to other room plans.

Repetition of a specific element or an idea is usually the most successful way to achieve transition. Popular methods include repeating a particular theme or mood; a floor covering; a furniture style; or a specific design element, such as a color, a type of texture, or a pattern motif. More than one of these repetitions can be used within one dwelling. However, open-plan areas usually should be esthetically designed as one room and a comfortable visual transition provided between adjacent rooms. Although each room is uniquely planned, all rooms within a home should appear to belong together.

Architectural changes and improvements involve any type of construction that in some way alters the basic structure of the home. These alterations include major changes such as room additions, the removal of interior walls, or a complete **renovation** of a room. Or the work can be less complicated—for example, relocating a door or adding or removing a window. Certain architectural improvements involve not only basic structural changes but also changes in other details, such as plumbing or electricity. Therefore, because architectural changes might affect the remainder of the room's design, they should be determined early in the designing stage.

While interior design is basically concerned with the effects of architectural changes on the *interior* plans, it is also important to recognize the potential benefits of exterior alterations to the total design plan. For example, relocating the front door could provide a separate entry hall

161

in the interior. Or minor changes in the exterior styling of the home might better integrate the exterior design with the interior.

Most interior architectural changes involve "opening up" or increasing space within a home, such as removing a wall or enlarging a room. However, a room plan may be improved by "closing off" space. For example, an open-plan living-dining room may be divided to separate the areas, or a large, poorly arranged kitchen can be reorganized to create a space for informal entertainment as well as an area for meal preparation and service.

It may be difficult for you to determine when structural changes should and can be made in your own environment. If you feel that there are some changes that could be beneficial, it would be helpful for you to arrange a consultation with an architect or an interior designer who also specializes in architectural planning. Since architectural changes are costly, the potential benefits should be evaluated in relation to the cost.

Throughout the television programs for this telecourse you have been introduced to a number of professional interior designers. You have heard them discussing their work and seen them working with clients in a systematic manner to create home environments which are esthetically and psychologically pleasing and functionally satisfying. Each of these designers brings his or her own personality and personal style to a rewarding and challenging profession. If the experience of this telecourse has aroused or reinforced your interest in interior design as a career, the last chapter of your text will provide information and suggestions to help you further explore this possibility.

LEARNING OBJECTIVES

After reading the assignment, viewing the program, and completing the assigned activities, you will be able to accomplish the following objectives:

Comprehension Objectives

1. Define the term "transitional flow" and identify at least three ways to achieve visual and psychological transition throughout a dwelling.
2. Describe three ways architectural changes can enhance an overall design plan.
3. Define the roles and responsibilities of an interior designer and describe the career opportunities and required training for this field.
4. Explain the role of computer technology in interior design.

Skill Objectives

1. Arrange in sequential order a list of steps to be included in the development of a total room.
2. Suggest two architectural changes for a room or home and explain how each could improve the total design.

ASSIGNMENTS

Before Viewing the Program

- Review pages 289–325 and read pages 329–336 in the text, noting particularly those terms listed in the glossary in this lesson.
- Read the comprehension and skill objectives for this lesson in the study guide.

□ Carefully study the overview, highlighting the important points and new concepts.

□ Look over the study activities and study questions for this lesson.

View the Program "Pulling It All Together"

While viewing the program, note specifically:

□ architectural interior designers Jackie Olmstead and Jan Neville illustrating that "camouflage remodeling" and relative simple architectural changes can transform the interior and exterior appearance of a home.

□ that architectural harmony and eclectic styling contribute to transitional flow.

□ the logical sequence of work from beginning to completion of remodeling, renovation, or interior design.

□ that transitional flow is psychological as well as visual.

After Viewing the Program

□ Review the glossary terms and learning objectives.

□ Complete the study activities.

□ Test your understanding of this lesson by answering the study questions at the end of the lesson. Check your answers with the key.

GLOSSARY

(Page numbers refer to your text.)

architectural or structural changes, study guide overview

commercial-contract designer, page 331

design specialist, page 331

design journalist, page 331

drafter, page 331

renderer, page 331

renovation: restoring a home to a previous quality or condition.

sequential work plan: the logical sequence of accompanying the work planned in a complete interior design plan.

set designer, page 331

STUDY ACTIVITIES

Required Activities

1. Using your present living environment or another furnished home, evaluate the use of transitional flow. Write a two-page paper identifying specific improvements that could be made.

2. Tour a newly constructed home and see how many major or minor architectural changes you feel would improve the overall plan. List these suggestions.

Extra-Credit Activities

1. Write a two-page paper discussing how to establish a good sequential plan for design implementations and two ways to achieve transitional flow.
2. Visit or write to a school of interior design or a college which offers a degree in this discipline. Ask about the entrance requirements, the course work, the expected completion time of the necessary training, and the job placement services offered by this institution. Write a two-page paper describing your findings.

STUDY QUESTIONS

(Select the one best answer.)

Comprehension Objective 1:   Define the term "transitional flow" and identify at least three ways to achieve visual and psychological transition throughout a dwelling.

1. Transitional flow is characterized by
   a. adjacent rooms that relate to each other.
   b. smooth eye movement from one room to another.
   c. an identical theme in each room of the house.
   d. all of the above factors.
   e. the factors described in a and b.

2. Which of the following is an effective way to create transitional flow throughout a home?
   a. Use the same size and shape windows throughout the home.
   b. Install the same wall-to-wall carpeting in every room.
   c. Repeat colors, patterns, and motifs throughout the home.
   d. Use the same ceiling treatment in each room.

3. Living in a home that has transitional flow will provide the benefit of
   a. a setting that is psychologically relaxing.
   b. a home that is easy to decorate.
   c. better scale and proportion throughout a home.
   d. uniformity of style in every room of the home.

Comprehension Objective 2:   Describe three ways architectural changes can enhance an overall design plan.

4. According to the television program, one way to make a room appear larger and more spacious through an architectural change is to
   a. add ceiling skylights.
   b. raise the ceiling.
   c. install a light-colored floor.
   d. paint the walls white.
   e. do all of the above.

5. Which of the following examples represent(s) (an) architectural change(s)?
   a. adding a closet
   b. removing a window
   c. installing a door
   d. changing the plumbing
   e. all of the above

6. Architectural changes should be motivated by
    a. the needs of the owners or occupants.
    b. the interior designer's wishes.
    c. a desire to have a truly unique home.
    d. economic factors.
    e. all of the above factors.

Comprehension Objective 3:   Define the roles and responsibilities of an interior designer and describe the career opportunities and required training for this field.

7. Which of the following is *not* required of an interior designer?
    a. clear and honest communication with clients
    b. ability to draw architectural renderings
    c. ability to work with an architect at all stages of a job
    d. knowledge of period and contemporary furniture and architecture
    e. concern with product durability

8. Which of the following are optional careers in interior design?
    a. owning a specialty shop or heading a design firm
    b. set designing or commercial design
    c. becoming a drafter or renderer
    d. all of the above
    e. the careers described in a and b

9. A person studying for a career in interior design could expect to _____ during the formal schooling period.
    a. develop communication skills
    b. learn about building codes
    c. study layout and space planning
    d. do all of the above
    e. pursue the training described in a and b

10. The field of interior design is relatively static.
    a. true
    b. false

Comprehension Objective 4:   Explain the role of computer technology in interior design.

11. Which of the following is *not* an advantage of using computers in interior design?
    a. saving time
    b. ability to consider a wide range of options
    c. personalized service to clients
    d. greater accuracy
    e. easy storage of client information

12. A computer allows a designer and a client to view a potential design in a variety of color schemes.
    a. true
    b. false

ANSWER KEY

(Page numbers refer to your text.)

1. e (study guide, television program)
2. c (study guide)
3. a (television program)
4. b (television program)
5. e (study guide, television program)
6. a (study guide, television program)

7. b (pages 329–331)
8. d (pages 331–332)
9. d (pages 330–331)
10. b (page 335)
11. c (pages 323–333)
12. a (page 332)